Retirement Planning

The Brief Guide to Lifelong Financial Freedom

(Retirement Planning Guide for Dummies and How to Make Your Money Last)

Heather Herman

Published By **Heather Herman**

Heather Herman

Retirement Planning: The Brief Guide to Lifelong Financial Freedom (Retirement Planning Guide for Dummies and How to Make Your Money Last)

ISBN 978-1-77485-444-0

Legal & Disclaimer

The information contained in this book is not designed to replace or take the place of any form of medicine or professional medical advice. The information in this book has been provided for educational and entertainment purposes only.

The information contained in this book has been compiled from sources deemed reliable, and it is accurate to the best of the Author's knowledge; however, the Author cannot guarantee its accuracy and validity and cannot be held liable for any errors or omissions. Changes are periodically made to this book. You must consult your doctor or get professional medical advice before using any of the suggested remedies, techniques, or information in this book.

Upon using the information contained in this book, you agree to hold harmless the Author from and against any damages, costs, and expenses, including any legal fees potentially resulting from the application of any of the information provided by this guide. This disclaimer applies to any damages or injury caused by the use and application, whether directly or indirectly, of any advice or information presented, whether for breach of contract, tort, negligence, personal injury, criminal intent, or under any other cause of action.

You agree to accept all risks of using the information presented inside this book. You need to consult a professional medical practitioner in order to ensure you are both able and healthy enough to participate in this program.

TABLE OF CONTENTS

Introduction

"There's a fountain of youth. This is your mind and talents and the creativity you bring in your life. Once you are able to tap into this source, age will vanish.

Sophia Loren

Everybody dreams about retirement. You've spent your adult lives saving, working, and sometimes even putting off enjoying life in order to be ready for the golden years. You've done it. The end is coming! Your financial advisor is giving you a pat on the back. He or she wants you to accept that gold watch your coworkers gave you, and help you live your retirement dreams. So why are you feeling nervous?

Many people become more concerned about their retirement as the days approach. Realizing that retirement is more than your financial stability or financial health is a significant step in your life. While financial security is important, it's not the only thing that matters. New questions emerge such as, "Am I

1

emotionally ready to take my full retirement?" How can my active lifestyle be maintained? How can I ensure my healthcare needs are met in retirement? Should I leave my house and move? These are just a few of the many concerns you need to address as your retirement nears. The importance of preparing your whole lifestyle for retirement is equal to the effort you've put into financial planning over many years. Your mental, emotional and physical health will all impact how well you can spend the years you want to be "the best" in your life.

How will you adjust to your retirement lifestyle as you plan? You may have to be more careful about following a monthly budget. You might have to find other ways to keep your brain sharp without having to worry about the daily demands of your job. Sometimes, you might be pondering the question of "what am I going to do?" Maybe you have had this all along: no project deadlines and no work rush. Perhaps you imagined exotic vacations or staying up late, or simply the freedom to do whatever you like whenever you feel like it. It doesn't matter how you pictured spending your newfound freedom, retirement can be a surprise. New adventures, new challenges and even anxiety will all be presented.

Your entire working life has reinforced the belief that financial security is the main concern when you plan for retirement. Brokers, retirement advisors and financial institutions are geared towards the monetary side of your preparation to support yourself when you stop working. Even most literature on the topic of retirement focuses on investing to provide you financial security in your later years. Many people put a lot of effort into saving for their retirement funds, but don't think about other aspects of retirement. Avoiding other aspects of retirement planning such as investing and financial preparation is a big mistake.

You've purchased the ultimate guidebook, which will walk you through all aspects of your retirement planning. Contrary to what he or she may believe, there are more ingredients that will help seniors enjoy a comfortable, secure, and happy retirement. Planning is vital to continue a fulfilling life after you have finished your work. This book can help you get started on your journey to planning your retirement. You will be able to see the importance of your emotional, mental and social well-being after you retire.

You've done a tremendous job up to now, and your smart financial decisions and dedication have allowed you to enjoy the latter years of your life without the stress and expectations that come with formal employment. Prepare yourself for this new chapter by making preparations in other areas of life. One out of every eight Americans are 65 years or older. These older people are in better financial and physical health than previous generations and can enjoy a wide range of options to maintain a happy, fulfilled life. All you need to do is be prepared.

Chapter 1: Retirement Planning

For a smooth transition into retirement, here are some pre-planning strategies and tips

"A gold timepiece is the perfect gift for retirement since its recipients have given so many of those golden hours in a life of service."

Terri Guillemets

You are at the point in you career where you are fast approaching the age when you want to retire. You have approximately 2 to 5 years of working experience, so you can transition into retirement. A majority of employees are dissatisfied or bored with their job, which is why many want to retire as soon as they can. Satisfaction surveys among those in the workforce show that this trend has been evident. Willis Towers Watson conducted a survey of more than 5,000 workers to find that 46 percent expect to reach age 65 before they retire. When it comes to retirement, 65 is a common number.

Retirement at the End of Your Life

65: The average age at 65 is considered ideal. According to 24% of respondents, 65 was the most popular. This is largely due to the ease of signing up for Medicare. Employers no longer have to cover you. One important side note: After the end World War II, baby boomers aren't eligible for full Social Security benefits. They were born between 1946-64. Accordingly, signing up to social security at 65 when you retire will decrease your monthly social insurance income by approximately 7%. People born after 1960 are required to wait to be 67 in order to receive full Social Security benefits. This means that if they decide to retire, enrolling in social safety at 65 would reduce their monthly income by around 13 percent.

70: Seventy seems to be the second most popular age at which to retire. According the study, one quarter of the workers surveyed stated that they intend to work until reaching this age. These retirees can collect more social security benefits if they wait until they turn 70. This is 32 percent more than the retirement age of 65. Social security checks for those born after 1960 would increase by 24%. Even though this is true, many people working in the workforce are not physically able to delay retirement until age 70. Health issues can force some people to retire earlier than expected.

Ages 66 to69: 18% said they were planning on retiring between 66, 69 and 70. This is a natural time frame since they would be eligible to claim Medicare and all social security benefits. They could withdraw their retirement income without a penalty, but they are not required yet to begin with withdrawing from personal retirement savings.

Age 62-64. 11 percent of those surveyed predicted that they will retire between the ages 65 and 62. These individuals will be able to get reduced social benefits, but they won't be eligible Medicare. Instead they will need to purchase their own insurance until they reach age 65. Some employers will cover health care for retired employees until they qualify for Medicare coverage.

Setting a specific retirement age will encourage you to get started on this new stage in your life. The stress of retirement can be reduced by having a plan in place. You will also have the opportunity to work on the steps toward retirement in smaller increments.

After you have determined your retirement age, you must now consider your living conditions. It is smart to begin to consider your housing and living requirements before you retire. You will be better equipped to predict your financial needs in retirement. There are many factors to consider before making a decision whether to move into a new home, apartment or senior living community.

Housing Options during Retirement

Deciding what you do with your home can be daunting and overwhelming. Depending on your housing situation, you might decide to stay or to sell your home. You may choose to live in an apartment, move into a senior living community for retired people with active lifestyles, or share your home with a spouse or child. The opportunities are plentiful and there are many choices to choose from.

If you do not currently own your home, your choices about your living arrangements will change. If this is the case, however, you will not need to sell your residence. However, you might consider what your ultimate goal is. You will be able to stay in the current apartment for a specified period. You should plan to end your current lease at the conclusion of your contract. You can rent another apartment, move to a retirement facility, or purchase a new home. It is important to weigh all the options and take into account their financial, as well as emotional, and even physical effects. Take a look at the terrain around your current apartment building. Is your home easily accessible via an elevator from the ground-floor or stairs? You might be happy where you are right now. But, think about what you will need as you age and how you can make your space work for you.

We'll be discussing in detail options related to retirement living. This includes selling an existing property and other important aspects. This will allow you to envision your future life. If you plan on traveling often, such as to exotic destinations or to visit with your children and grandchildren frequently or for longer periods of times, ask yourself these questions. Ask yourself if you are currently paying off your home mortgage or if you plan on doing so in retirement. It will probably be a major factor in your ability or inability to leave your current home. This can also impact your ability/ability to move to a better location. Many homeowners will be retiring soon, and are looking to reduce the amount of space they need to raise their families. Others cannot fathom moving out of the home they shared with young children. These homeowners choose to keep their homes for as long and as they feel good.

Selling Your Home

A great option for retirees is to list their home for sale. If you are the owner of your home or have significant equity, you may be able to sell it to help meet your retirement planning needs. As long as you lived in your home for at most two years, or five years, before you sell it, you can deduct up to $250,000 and $500,000 of the capital gain. If your finances are struggling and the local housing market is healthy, this might be a good option.

Selling your home could also be an option if it becomes more difficult for you to navigate the home with your age. If you have additional needs, stairways, which can be long and difficult to navigate within the house, as well as parking spaces or garages that lead to the front door, could become a problem.

It is possible that you are considering moving to a different area or country in order to retire. To make sure that it's the perfect location for you to retire, you might want to sell your home and rent out the space.

It is important to assess your ability and financial resources to continue paying your mortgage (if you have a mortgage), as well as the expenses that you will still need to maintain your home. The greater the age of your house, the more maintenance you will have to do. As with your time and finances, the bigger your house is, both financially and in terms of its impact on your life. Another financial obligation that you should consider is the cost to pay for utilities. Your extra space may no longer be needed for family gatherings or visits from grandchildren or grandchildren. The fact that these extra rooms are still used, no matter how often, means that you will continue to have to heat and cool the rest of your home. In addition, property taxes will be added to the overall size of the house. A prime location may have been the one you sought when you bought your house. It might have offered the best schools, the most convenient shopping, and the best neighborhood. These perks may not have been essential for you at this time in your life. However, your property tax will still reflect these perks. If you are considering retiring, consider how you might be able use the extra funds that your large house requires for other areas of your lifestyle. Consider these benefits before you decide if this is the right choice for your circumstances.

Staying at Your Current Home

When you decide to move, your goal is most likely to either rent or buy smaller properties with the money that you get from selling your home. If your goal is to rent, then you'll have to pay money that you'll never receive a return. Some people feel it's a better financial decision not to rent but to maintain their home.

This decision will depend on how much equity you have in your home. If you don't have a home mortgage anymore (or are just about to pay it off), you will need to evaluate the expenses for your home. These include average maintenance costs, taxes, fees, upkeep, and taxes. The cost of buying a smaller house in cash or renting an apartment. If your home has low equity, or you're not close to purchasing the home, you might reconsider staying.

If the value of your property has been increasing, staying put in your house for even a few more years may prove to be advantageous. It all depends on how the market is in your area. You might want to speak with a real agent to see if you can benefit financially by keeping your house for several years.

There are many reasons retirees might choose to live in their homes even though they may not be financially motivated. Some couples may have been living in their home all their lives. Your satisfaction as a retiree may be directly affected by the emotional attachment you feel to your home. This is another reason to maintain a home, provided that they are financially able.

There is no one-size fits all approach to retirement planning. These aspects should be evaluated before you officially retire. If you're faced with a tough decision, especially regarding whether to sell your home or keep it, it may be useful to reflect on the benefits and disadvantages of each option. Get your financial information together and calculate your projected monthly income using your investments and social insurance checks. Next, make a list of the costs associated with each option. You can either rent or buy a smaller home. If you choose to stay in your home, pay the taxes, maintenance, and mortgage. This information will impact your decision greatly and will allow to you to concentrate on the positives in your new situation. Look at the many benefits to downsizing. It can lead to greater financial freedom, more free time, and you can also celebrate the chance to continue living your life in the company of the memories of your kids that enrich your emotional well-being.

Senior Living Options

There is a wide range of senior-specific housing and living options today to suit active retirees. People associate senior living with the word "nursing home". In this setting, elderly people are treated like patients and receive medically-trained care. This is a good option for retirees who need to live in a safe environment. But there are other communities that can accommodate active aging individuals without any or medical help. These communities, known as independent or active living, are ideal for older adults over 55 who want to keep their independence while also having easy access transportation services, social events, and cleaning and laundry assistance. Each community offers different services. It is important to think about the amenities you are interested in, before you make a decision on which community you would like to live in. Some communities provide only a few services to maintain residents' social activities. This could be a retired-specific community that offers a fitness center, clubhouse, landscaping and maintenance services, as well a social calendar. Other communities might offer more comprehensive services, including transportation, meal options, housekeeping, laundry, security, and even housekeeping. The community offers a range of on-site benefits, including some that are more or less costly, for anyone interested in this type of retirement living.

Assisted living communities are similar in concept to active communities but cater to seniors who need assistance with their daily lives. People living in assisted living communities have greater access to aid, including personal hygiene and transportation services, as well as medical assistance. These communities can be a great option for seniors or those with partners who are suffering from an ongoing medical condition.

Relocating for Retirement

It's a good idea to think about where you will be moving when you retire. You might find yourself a few years from starting your retirement. Perhaps you're dreaming of the freedoms offered by it. You may have even considered that this newfound freedom might enable you to live wherever you choose. Bankrate, a consumer-financial services company, discovered that half of all adults aged between 50 and 64 said they would consider moving after their retirement.

This percentage drops down to 20% for those over 64. Statistically, most retirees decide to remain where they are comfortable and enjoy their retirement. Some people see retirement as an opportunity to get up and move. However, thoughtful planning is necessary when choosing a final destination.

Considerations such as financial and logistical issues, as well as quality of life, are important aspects to consider when choosing a retirement spot.

Before you consider moving, make sure to research the tax laws in that specific state or country. It's important to learn about the state's death, sales and income taxes. It's possible you might move to a state with higher or lower rates for each of these expenses. If this happens, you should be aware of how it will affect your budgeted earnings. Georgia, for instance, allows you to receive an income exemption on your social security benefits. This makes Georgia appealing to retired persons. Vermont, on the other hand, doesn't allow for any exemptions to retirement income. This state is also one 13 that taxes your social benefits. Certain states may offer tax breaks to seniors such as lower sales taxes, higher property taxes, or forgoing estate and inheritance tax. These are all benefits that could be advantageous to retirees. In general, tax laws in states that appeal to many citizens can be compensated for by other means that could still have an impact on you. Oregon residents do, however, not pay a sales or use tax. The estate tax levied upon included assets has a maximum value of $1,000,000, far less than the government's applicable bracket for estate taxes, which is $5.43million.

While taxes are an important consideration for retirement, it is also important not allow your final decision to be influenced solely by taxes. In truth, this is the only criterion that would influence your relocation decision. You could be packing to Alaska! It is free of income and sales taxes. All residents who have lived in the state more than one year are eligible for a dividend from an oil reserve. These checks are approximately $1,500 each year, though the exact amount can change every year. Alaska's cost per capita is higher than any other state due to increased costs for housing, groceries, utilities, health care, and high-priced food items. Although this is a very extreme example, it illustrates the importance of considering all costs associated to living in a given area. It also highlights how costly it is to relocate.

In addition to the overall cost of living in the new area (home prices, income tax costs and utility expenses), you must also take into account the travel costs you will incur to visit family members or get medical treatment. This is particularly crucial when deciding on a move. You are likely to disengage yourself from the support system you have built in your local area over the years that you live there. This is why many retirees remain in the same area.

The weather is another factor that can seem quite trivial but is crucial to take into account when you make a decision about relocating. It's important that you become familiar with the climate throughout the year in the area. Consider this: If you haven't been to Florida in the summer, you may not be aware that the region is hot and prone to mosquito bites. It would be a shock to move to Florida based upon your perceptions of the place during winter vacations only to find out that you are not equipped to handle the hot summer weather.

It is important to evaluate the accessibility of key matters such as health care facilities, volunteering opportunities, and your proximity to loved-ones when visiting potential retirement areas.

CNBC conducted a study to rank the best and most expensive states to retire. They looked at the state's financial, quality, and healthcare factors and how they impact retirees. This list may be helpful if there are many options for you to consider when making a move.

Budgeting to Save for Retirement

If you're anything like most people, you may be feeling less than enthusiastic about this section's message and content. Surprisingly a budget can make your mental well-being better by decreasing stress and increasing enjoyment. Although it is hard to believe that budgeting can help you make more money for things you enjoy, and keep you from making costly mistakes during retirement. There are many factors that will impact your financial future, including Social Security, parttime income, inflation rate, return on investment, retirement date, taxes, and healthcare spending. There are many factors that you cannot control, but your deliberate and calculated spending is something that you can influence. If you put in the effort now, you can take control of your retirement budget and make smart decisions about the lifestyle you want. It is possible to save money on your retirement budget by making some compromises and adjustments. You may find you are able to travel more, retire early, or spend more of your time enjoying your hobbies.

How to set aside a budget for retirement

It is important to start by compiling the required information.

* One-year worth of bank account statements
* Credit card statements that last one year
* Two of your most recent pay stubs.
* There are approximately 10 highlighters in different colors
* Your tax return from the last year

These items are reviewed to find out where your money is. Next, you will use the highlighters for creating groups of expenses within different categories.

Step 1: Fixed Costs

At the very beginning, list all your expenses that repeat on a monthly, annual, or quarterly basis. This list should then be divided into three sections:

* Essential expenses: Food and clothing, housing costs, transport costs, and healthcare
* Non-essential expenses include cable TV, gym membership, monthly subscription services, and additional monthly expenses that do not need to be met.

* These are expenses that you must pay monthly but not monthly. They include items like vehicle registration, vehicle registration, insurance policies, and property taxes. It is important to keep track of the monthly cost for these items so that you can add them to your monthly budget.

TIP: Use a 12 month spreadsheet to account of fluctuating spending across the year. Each expense will be listed at the bottom of the page. If you spent $600 during holidays to buy gifts, add "gifts" to the expense line and write $600 below the month of December. If your monthly electric bill is $150 or more, add the expense category "electric bill" and note $150 on each month.

Step 2: Inflating Healthcare Costs

If you are a retiree, you could lose the employer-paid health insurance premium and be forced to pay the cash. If you're planning to retire before age 65, you can expect your insurance premiums to be close to $1,000 per month. To properly budget this expense, you should start shopping around. Be sure to include healthcare costs such as hearing, vision, and dental that are not covered by traditional medical insurance. To calculate the cost of living, it is important to have an idea of how much money you anticipate spending on these items.

Step 3: Optional Charges

This section should include any expenses that you wish to pay, like entertainment, travel, or fun.

Step 4 Lifestyle Considerations

You will need to think about what changes you could expect to your hobbies and life style (as a married couple). What do you plan to do with your retirement years? Do you have an expensive hobby or plan on continuing it? You'll need to make sure that you budget more money for expensive hobbies. You may find that there are lifestyle changes you are willing to make to allow more money to be spent on the things you care about most. If you have a strong desire to travel, you may need to downsize to be able to move money from one area to another.

Step 5 Fix vs. Flex

1. Add all your expenses
2. Total fixed expenses separately
3. Divide the fixed expenses in half to get the total expense

This will enable you to calculate how much (or not) of your retirement income is going to be used to cover fixed expenses. You will need to take into account this number, and how it impacts step 4. This is the part of your retirement budgeting plan that will determine how you want your time to be spent. This is where large monthly expenses like a car or house payment will be addressed and how they can be reduced to allow for more funds for your hobbies and travel.

If you want to spend more time enjoying retirement, it is important to reduce or eliminate your fixed expenses. You'll be able to use the money you have to pay for activities that you enjoy.

After you have calculated your expenses, and created a budget for yourself, what can you do if the expenses seem to outweigh your income. To help you prepare for retirement, it is crucial that you determine what changes you can make to your lifestyle that will allow you to live within your budget once you are done working.

Consider a few options before you retire that will reduce your monthly expenditures without having an adverse effect on your quality life.

* Relocate to lower cost areas: If the housing market is experiencing a significant increase in price, you might consider moving to an area that has not been affected as much. It depends on where your current residence is and the location you're moving to, it may be possible to dramatically reduce your monthly expenses in the areas of insurance, maintenance, tax, and other living expenses. Imagine a retiree who is able to make $300,000. He could have built equity over the years and gotten a steady income from the rising market. After moving to a more affordable area and investing that profit, he is able to save money on his monthly expenses while still

generating income through the interest from the investment. It is possible to keep your current home but downsize without sacrificing your ability to live there. This would allow you the freedom to cut back on expenses that could be burdensome for your post-retirement income.

* Pay your mortgage off: This can help simplify your cash flow as well as reduce financial stress. This is the pre-retirement phase. You should research the benefits of refinancing the mortgage. If you are unable to do so, increase your monthly mortgage payments.

* Get rid off all debt. Not only are they draining on your monthly income, but they also add to the cost of interest. This is something that you should be earning and not paying during this stage of retirement planning.

* Evaluate expenses. Use this opportunity to examine all your expenses and eliminate the ones that are unnecessary. As you move closer to retirement, you may feel that additional cars, second

homes, memberships to professional associations or clubs are less important.

* Assess your insurance. You might no longer need to have life or disability coverage depending on how near your retirement date. This is an opportunity to reduce unnecessary expenses at this stage in your lives and make your budget more efficient.

Other general preparations to be retired soon

The following items will help you make a smooth transition into retirement.

Estate Planning: Your years spent building up your financial wealth and getting everything organized so you can enjoy retirement. These terrible possibilities are something that no one likes to think about. If your estate is not well planned, you will likely lose a significant amount of your assets, such as attorney fees, taxes and probate costs. You should have your lawyer review your will. These items must be kept current to ensure that they fit your life stage.

Documents If that day comes, someone will have to manage your affairs. It will be so much more beneficial for them if your important documents are organized and stored in a clearly identified place. It may be worth adding:

* A listing of all financial account numbers with contact information. Any financial accounts that you receive statements for such as loans and life insurance, investments or annuities will be added to this list.
* Wills. Powers of attorney, medical directives. Trust documents.
* Marriage certificate
* Burial instructions
* Deeds of property, including vehicle titles
* Documents pertaining to the military
* An itemized checklist of valuables

Be Healthy. You've worked for your whole life to make enough money to have the time you need. A heart attack or debilitating disease can limit your ability and enjoyment of what you've worked so hard to achieve. It can make your retirement more satisfying by focusing on your health in these final years of life.

Prepare Your Home: If your goal is to downsize or relocate, you should begin to clean out and declutter your home. Make any repairs that may affect the value of your home. Although you may have lived in the house for at least 20 years, it's unlikely that you'll be moving out within a few months.

Financial Advisors: It is possible to have a second opinion, for a fee, from a financial advisor. This will ensure that you are not making any mistakes in your retirement plans. Ask your advisor questions about your retirement plans before making any final decisions.

* Monthly payments vs. lump Sum from Pensions

* Are you ready to get Social Security benefits now or should you wait?

* Should you get long-term healthcare insurance?

* Medi-gap coverage as opposed to self-insuring

* Which accounts should you use to start withdrawing money and in what order?
* Converting savings for annuity
* How much are your savings allowed to be withdrawn each year?
* How can your assets be arranged to benefit your descendants?

You're now in the final stretch of your working career. The next few year will give you the opportunity to smoothen the transition into retirement.

Chapter 2: Financial Considerations

Maximizing Social Security and understanding your Pension Options

"Retirement - It's nice not to be in the ratrace but you also have to learn to live with less cheese."

Gene Perret

Maximizing Social Security

Most people think that once they have become eligible for Social Security, they will be able to simply sign paperwork and begin collecting the amount due them for the lifetime of contributing to it. In reality, it is more complicated. You have this opportunity to better understand the process, so that you get the most out of the benefits you are entitled when you collect.

Social Security Program has over 2,700 rules and stipulations. Even the most diligent person could easily get overwhelmed by all of the information. There are many ways you can maximize your Social Security payment. This depends on your marital status, your income while working and your financial situation. The following are key points that will help you maximize your social safety benefits.

1. Waiting is okay. You can start receiving your benefits as soon as you turn 62. However, it is worth understanding that the more you wait, both you and your spouse will get less. If you delay collecting benefits until you reach 70 years old, you will get 76% more than if they were available at 62. For every year you delay retirement, you are entitled to a credit equaling 8% per year plus inflation. Deferment credits stop once you reach 70. You can't wait to start collecting benefits after that age.

2. Know which benefits you are eligible: If you are married or widowed and/or divorced, it may be possible to get a "spousal", "survivor", or "spousal " benefit. These benefits have three components. They include the length of your marriage, how long you wait to remarry, as well as when you apply.

You or your spouse can collect the full spousal advantage if you're married. It is half of the other's retirement benefit.

If you and your spouse are divorced, you can each collect a spousal income amount that is dependent on the other party's retirement benefit. As long as you were married for at most 10 years.

If you're widowed, you can receive a survivor's bonus. This could be the full amount for your deceased spouse's retirement benefit. However, it depends on when and how much you apply.

3. Only claim one benefit at a given time. For example, if your situation gives you the opportunity to receive a retirement benefits plus a survivor advantage, you may lose one of those benefits if you try to claim them all at once. In such situations, you are only allowed to claim the largest of the benefits. The best option is to first receive the smaller benefit and claim it later.

For example, if your spouse dies before you become eligible for your own benefits, then you could collect both your own retirement and survivor benefits. The downside is that you can't cash in on both your retirement benefit and survivor benefits at the same time. You will only receive one payout for the rest. Therefore, it would be in your interest to understand the correct strategy to receive all benefits. If you decide to cash in on both benefits simultaneously, you should claim your own retirement benefit at age 62 (let's assume $1800), and then file for your survivor payments once you reach age 66 (assuming this is your full retirement date). Your survivor payout will be equal in value to the full amount of the deceased spouse's due payments (let us say $2,469). Then, you will be able to collect $1800 per month over a period 4 years and then $24,469 per year for the rest your life. This is a 23% greater payment, starting at age 66 and ending on the day you are born.

4. Filing and Suspension. Your spouse cannot collect spousal benefits if they have not filed for them. If you want to hold off on collecting your own benefits and wait until you turn 70, you may file for

your benefits as soon as you reach full retirement age. Otherwise, you will be able to suspend the collection of your benefits until your 70th birthday. Your spouse can also claim their benefit by waiting until age 70.

5. Divorce is possible if you have been married more than 10 year. Both you and your spouse are eligible to claim your Spousal Benefit. This allows you to delay the collection of retirement benefits so that you can reach the maximum monthly allowance at 70. Divorced can have the advantage of being married. However, a married couple cannot claim more than one spousal, while a spouse can claim an additional spousal. For both benefits to be available, one must have been divorcing for at least two consecutive years. You must be at minimum 62 years of age to file, or your ex spouse must be eligible for disability benefits.

6. Remarrying might reduce your benefits. This is because if you divorce before 60 years, and you remarry, your spousal spousal payments from your ex-spouse's

record are not available. This is true even if your spouse has died. Also, if you marry before 60 you lose the survivor benefit. If you marry after the age of 60, your survivor and/or spousal benefits will continue to be available.

7. Some benefits of being married include the fact that you are more likely to get social security payouts than someone who is always single. If you are married for less than 12 months, you will be entitled to a spouse benefit. You may also receive a survivor advantage if your spouse is still alive after you have been married for nine months.

For example: If you want your married couple to get the most out of their social security benefits, it might be a good idea to set up a collection plan. Your wife may retire early and receive a smaller benefit. You (her husband) can file for a spouse benefit based off your wife's retirement benefits once you reach your full retirement years (66 or 67). Once your husband reaches 70 years old, you can begin receiving your own benefits. The effectiveness of your plan will depend on how much you earn and when you retire.

It can be hard to know how to get the best out of your social safety and maximize your payouts. There are many options available for filing. Additionally, there are thousands upon thousands of requirements. These seven basic tips will help maximize your benefits. However there are many other factors that may apply depending on your unique situation. These strategies will increase your income from social security. But, there are tools to help you create a step by-step filing plan.

Social Security Solutions (a software and educational company) is dedicated to ensuring its clients receive the maximum amount of Social Security payments. While they charge a fee for their services, they remove the guesswork from determining when and how to file social security. After consulting with them, they will evaluate your unique situation and recommend multiple filing methods to obtain your benefits. An exact plan will be provided for you. It will explain how and when you file for your benefits. If reading through thousands upon thousands of rules and stipulations to make sure you aren't missing out is too much for you, it might be worth seeking guidance from a qualified advisor.

Also, the government's Social Security website offers an estimation calculator which can give you an idea about the benefits you might receive based on the records of your earnings through Social Security. This estimator is able provide an approximate calculation but will not produce the actual amount of collectible benefit. This is due to the possibility that your wages may rise or fall in the future. Also, once you start receiving benefits, they will be adjusted for inflation.

Understanding Your Retirement

If your employer offers a pension, you can choose to receive a lump-sum or monthly payment.

The length of your service as an employee will influence whether you receive a retirement payment. The size of the pension payment will vary depending on how long you were employed by a company.

Once you reach the age where you intend to retire, it is necessary to contact the division responsible for pensions at the company in order to receive your benefits. Technically, you can't claim your pension checks until you reach full pension age. But depending on the details of your company pension benefit, you may still be eligible for early retirement benefits. Be aware that your pension payments will be reduced if you claim them before you reach full-time retirement age. This is similar to Social Security.

When you are nearing retirement, another decision you will need is whether you would like to receive monthly annuities or a lump-sum pension. It doesn't matter which option is better for you.

Most people prefer to receive pension payments in monthly installments, or a Life Annuity. A steady stream is better for retirement than a large cash payment, especially if it's not easy to invest. Your propensity to overspend and spend too quickly can make it difficult to get your pension payment in the future. Some people may find it advantageous to receive their pension payment all at one time.

The first benefit to assuming full control of your pension is that you won't need to worry about the health or strength of your company. This reduces the chance of you losing money if your company goes bust or has to close its doors. If you opt to receive monthly payments but your company runs short of cash and closes down, you will lose any remaining money. The Pension Benefits Guarantee Corporation provides protection for some companies. They can recover some of your benefit earnings if you go bankrupt, but it is not guaranteed or required to.

Investors with experience will enjoy the second benefit of all the money being available at once. Once you have all the money, you are able to decide how to spend it and where to invest it. If you have the ability to manage the money efficiently, you may be able receive interest income for the rest your life.

If you have full control of your pension, you can give the money to your loved ones. If you have managed your money carefully, you can end up with enough money to sustain you for the rest of your retirement. You also might be left with a sum to pass on to your children and grandchildren.

If you do decide that you want to take your pension in one payment, it might be advantageous to then invest the remainder in your annuity. In this situation, you would collect your lumpsum payment, roll that money into an IRA, use part of the IRA for an "immediate anuity" from an insured company. When you invest in an immediate annuity, you can expect to receive income right away. This allows you to stabilize your stream of income just as you would if you chose to receive monthly pension payment. However, the final decision on the amount is up to you. This will give you the advantages of stable monthly income.

However, you also have the advantage of taking responsibility for all of your pension. Your company won't lose any of their benefit money until they pay it out. The other benefit of this plan? You will always have cash on hand in case something happens or you need it to keep up to date with inflation.

Consider two options for annuity payments monthly from your pension: a single or joint life annuity. A single-life annuity will pay out for the rest of you life. A joint or survivor annuity pays for your entire life. You will receive a monthly payment that is more if you choose to have a single annuity. However, the payout period for joint survivor annuities will typically be shorter. It is important to get the estimates from your company before you decide on the amount of your pension. It is possible to get a joint survivor and pension payout if your retirement savings are low. This will help ensure your spouse will have financial support after your death.

Always ensure you fully understand which payout option is best for your situation (and your money). For you, it is irrevocable.

Chapter 3: Managing Your Wellness

To bridge the gap in Medicare eligibility eligibility and retirement, consider getting health insurance

Many people are influenced greatly by the availability or lack thereof of health insurance options when planning for retirement. Retirementes under 65 who don't qualify for Medicare or are still paying the premiums for private insurance and health care can face a significant financial burden. A plan must be in place for your healthcare, prescription, and retirement planning. The Affordable Care Act (currently in effect) regulates how private insurance companies can charge seniors high premiums. They also have the right to refuse coverage for you if you have a condition.

The best option for early retirees will be the ability to continue the coverage that you were receiving through your employer. Although this option is rarer, many companies and government entities still offer it to early retirementes. In this instance, you would remain covered under the group plan used by your employer for their active employees. This usually has a time period attached with it, with enough leeway to allow for you to reach age 65 and qualify to Medicare. Most of the time, your premium would stay the exact same as it was while working for the company. While it isn't required by law, most companies will offer a spouse's plan if it was available in your policy while you were employed.

A second option is for you provide your own private insurance coverage by making use of the insurance exchange options. They were created in 2010 under the Affordable Health Care Act. This market provides coverage for individuals. Insurance companies are limited in their ability to deny coverage for certain conditions. You can sign-up at any time during the year (not only during open enrollment), as retirement and a loss in coverage are qualifiers. Sign ups can be made from 60 to 60 calendar days prior your retirement date, or as soon as you are ready.

It is usually the least expensive option for bridging the age gap between your work and retirement is to extend your employer's COBRA coverage for upto 18 months. Your entire coverage cost will be yours, with your company able to charge an administrative fee of 2%. This is an expensive and short-term option. If you have more than 1.5 years until you reach Medicare eligibility, you may need to look for another type of coverage.

Individuals can get tax credits for paying for premiums if they meet specific income criteria. The first step is to estimate your income after you retire. You can then apply for tax credits based on how much you pay for health coverage in your community. This option can make insurance more affordable if you plan on retiring prior to 65. Important: If your employer offers retiree healthcare coverage, you will most likely not be eligible to receive a tax credit.

It's a good idea to review your current life policy. Most people consider life insurance a backup plan that provides income to their spouse in case one of them dies. When there is no income available to replace it, it's a smart decision to end life insurance. It is important to evaluate your financial situation before cancelling any policy. There may be occasions when you are able to continue to pay your premium for life insurance even after the age of 60.

Consider your requirements for life insurance. Also, consider the cost of your current plan. It is possible that your premium might rise after reaching a certain age. However, this will depend on the details of your coverage. You may be able, depending on the terms of your policy, to switch to a more affordable policy that still provides benefits in the unlikely event of your death. In either event, cancelling your policy is a bad idea. It will affect your ability to renew the policy.

You might consider keeping your life insurance policy even if it is not necessary. It is a good idea for you to get a term insurance policy that has enough coverage to cover your credit balance if you're still paying a large amount of debt. If you don't already have a plan and want to ensure that your family is left with enough money for your debts after your death, you can purchase a term life policy. This policy will expire at your debt payment due date.

Chapter 4: Are Your Ready For Full Time Retirement?

Considerations to prepare for the transition out

"Half our lives are spent trying and find something to replace the time we have spent trying desperately to save."

Will Rogers

People spend years dreaming about their retirement plans, dreams, and the projects or hobbies they would enjoy. People envision all the adventures they have always wanted, but never had enough time for. Surprisingly a lot of people in the workforce who are about to retire find themselves questioning what their emotional plans for retirement look like.

You've worked hard over the years to save money and invest in financial preparation to be able one day to enjoy the things you have earned. Many people overlook the fact that their emotional preparedness is what is really staring them in a face. Your emotional and mental readiness is a state. It's possible to make the transition smoother by validating your concerns.

Start by asking yourself this question: "What are my plans for the future?" After considering how many hours worked at work, and whether you commuted or worked from home, you will be able to determine how much time there is to enjoy retirement. It is important to find hobbies and new opportunities to fill your life and keep you occupied. Volunteering and other charitable opportunities are common ways that retirees fill up some of their time. Hobbies like gardening and golf are all popular retirement activities. Others choose to continue their work in a different area of the economy, or take on part-time jobs. This option can keep your mind busy and help you learn new skills. Plus, it provides extra income. Be aware that your benefits could be severely reduced if the income you earn per year exceeds the maximum earning limit and you are younger than your full retirement. For every $2 you earn more than the allowed limit ($16,000.920) for 2017, your benefits will be reduced. You will lose $1 for every $3 earned in the year until you reach full pension age. If you were to retire in 2017, and continue working part-time, you would be allowed $44,880 per month. You can still work after your birthday and make as much money as you want, but your Social Security payment will not be reduced.

One question many retirees neglect to consider is: "How can we prepare to spend so many time together when we are so accustomed to being apart?" Even if you love and cherish your spouse, it will likely be a change in routines to spend most of your days in their company. It's a common experience that people have positive experiences with retirement-induced changes. But it's definitely something you'll want! Your partner and you can both benefit by taking up a hobby or an interest that is your own.

Many employees feel defined and defined by their careers. This might make you wonder "How can I give up my profession that is so important to me?". Sometimes, it feels like you have lost a part your identity. If you are used to your job title being part of your identity, it can be difficult to switch to a less demanding career. If you feel attached to your work and it becomes part of your identity, prepare for a period of adjustment where you might have difficulty "turning off" your work. This will allow you to enjoy your new relaxed lifestyle. Most retirees find fulfillment in their new low-stress lifestyle.

If you're a retired social butterfly and don't have the daily interaction you used to at work, you might worry about how your life will be without it. You may find that introverts are more comfortable with this change than others. If social interaction is something you enjoy, consider joining clubs and organizations in your community that provide opportunities to interact with others who have similar interests.

When people are emotionally prepared for retirement, they will feel able and capable of living a fulfilled and successful retirement.

Chapter 5: Seniors' Self-Care

Lifestyle changes to make for a happy retirement: Make them now!

The best retirement strategy to retire happy and prosperous

Don't put your burden on others.

Ernie Zelinski

After you have started saving money for retirement and are ready to retire, it's important to stay active about your health, financial and emotional well-being so you can fully enjoy the experience.

Your Physical Health

A lot of people will associate symptoms of side effects with prescription drugs or medical conditions and not the dangers of aging. Remaining objective about your general well-being as you age is key to ensuring that you have a fulfilling retirement.

You can start to make a fitness plan if you don't yet have one. To ensure that your daily routine can be continued after retirement, join a gym and/or take a daily stroll in the mornings or evenings. This will decrease the chances of you not following through on your fitness program after retirement.

You might consider starting a vitamin/supplement regimen, similar to what you do for your fitness. For aging bodies, calcium, iron antioxidants and B vitamin are all beneficial. However, you need to check with your doctor before using any vitamin or supplement. Many can interact with prescription drugs making them ineffective.

Do not think that you are simply getting older and experiencing sleep disturbances. It is true that people get more sleepless nights as they age.

While you're still working, ensure you take full advantage of the healthcare coverage that you have. You should visit your doctors on a regular basis, take your prescribed medication as instructed, and collaborate with your healthcare providers to resolve any lingering medical issues. The less money you have to spend on copays, prescription bills and office visits, the healthier you will feel when you retire. This is especially true if your retirement date falls before you are eligible for Medicare.

Mental Health

Your mental well-being is equally important to a fulfilling retirement. Your attitude can influence your physical health. Research has shown that people who believe certain diseases are unavoidable will have more of them than those who believe otherwise. This includes a decreased ability to remember and a longer recovery time from illnesses.

Your mental health is something you should address now. The lifestyle change that retirement brings can make these problems worse. These chapters will help you feel more prepared to retire, as well as reducing anxiety, stress, uncertainty, and other mental stressors.

Your Financial Health

Now is the time to make sure you keep your hard work and smart investments. Continue to invest and save for retirement up until the date you retire. If you haven't, follow this guide and start living on the budget.

Also, scams targeting retired and elderly individuals are very common in today's financial world. These frauds can cause serious financial damage to your retirement. The financial scam artists are responsible for approximately $3 billion in losses each year among seniors. [2] Avoid becoming a victim of financial fraud!

Common scams targeting seniors

Scammers calling Medicare Open Enrollment: Callers pretending to be from Centers for Medicare and Medicaid Services may make calls weeks prior to open enrollment for Medicare. They'll often state that they're working to issue new Medicare ID Cards and will require your bank information and Social Security numbers in order for you to verify your identity. The scammers will then use this information for withdraws from the bank account. Medicare will never call you, email you, visit or ask you for personal information.

Scammer targeting veterans in pensions: A scammer contacts vets over the age 65 and invites them for a free seminar. The seminar will teach them how to apply for the Aid and Attendance enhanced benefit to vets who have a low income and are disabled. Scammers will try convincing vets who do not qualify for the enhanced pension benefits, due to income restrictions, to change their financial circumstances in a way that only the scammers can benefit. Only get advice from the VA, or their list accredited professionals regarding your eligibility for Veteran's benefit.

Scammers are attempting to con seniors into selling (often by intimidation) stock markets that have been under traded in an attempt to artificially increase the share prices. As more senior citizens invest in the unprofitable stock, the share price keeps rising until stockbrokers sell their shares quickly and make a quick profit. Everyone else is left with no return. Be sure to do thorough research on any investment you make.

Take advantage of the years you have before retirement and make sure that you prepare for retirement. To reduce stress during this lifestyle transition, you need to protect your finances.

Chapter 6: The Importance Early Retirement

There is no specific time to retire. Instead, you have complete control over when and what you want. There are many jobs which have a retirement date. It varies from job to job and state-to-state. While retirement may appear easy, it is not always an easy task. In the end, you might have many regrets and worries. Even if you're not certain it will, you don't have to give up on retirement.

The winning strategy is what you use to prepare for retirement. Even though life is not always what we plan, we can reduce the chances of failure by creating the right strategy. Planning for retirement is a way to make sure your family has a good future in terms of wealth generation and investment management.

Many people want to work till they die, but others want to stop working so that they can retire early enough. Because you have the freedom to live the lifestyle you desire, it is essential to belong to the former. You can concentrate on your health, travel your dream destination and spend time doing what you love.

Although early retirement can be great in many ways it is not without its problems. Poor financial decisions taken before and during retirement are a major factor in early retirement. If you know how to create wealth and make it last, you can have a comfortable retirement.

Here we will examine the leading reasons why early retirement can be beneficial and what you need do to begin planning. If you are a veteran in your chosen field and you are considering retiring, these reasons may be useful.

1. The Average Life Expectancy of a Person is not Fixed

The greatest benefit to early retirement is in the realm of life expectancy. Over the years we have witnessed many changes in the life expectancy for workers. Many workers raised concerns that informed policies. These policies and the outcries of workers have been based on a simple fact: humans now live an average of three years longer. It is all due to technological progress that has improved health care by using sophisticated equipment.

Because the average life expectancy has been increasing, that means you have to provide more funds to enable you to retire comfortably. You won't work until your 80th birthday because the state's life expectancy average is this high. You will need financial planning to make sure you live comfortably.

You have the option to retire early and still be able do things you enjoy. If these things require your strength, it is even more important.

The average life expectancy is around 80 but many people live beyond that. If you are one of the lucky ones who will live beyond 80 years old, you will need to create a comprehensive retirement savings strategy to help you plan for longer. It allows you to plan for a life expectancy of around 80, but it also allows for you to make more plans and secure your old years.

2. There is a limit to the time you can work

No matter how good you feel, you can't keep working forever. There is a limit as to how long you may work and what kind of work you do. You will eventually lose efficiency if your ability to work for a longer time. As you age, there will be a decline in the quality and quantity of your efforts.

While working, you might find it difficult to put your mind on a retirement strategy other than that provided by your company. This is why so many people leave work and retire to live off what little they have. You can save more money by taking early retirement. You can save money by reducing the time and effort required to keep up with work.

Early retirement planning will help you save money, prepare you for, and sustain you throughout retirement. Without a comprehensive early retirement strategy, you may stay at work for a very long time.

3. It offers you the chance to carry out tasks that are on your bucket

It doesn't matter if your job is as an employee at a company, or as an entrepreneur working for you as your boss, you will have limited free time. Many people find it difficult to enjoy a 9-5 job. They feel that it takes up too much time and leaves them with very little or no time for other enjoyable things. It's just as difficult for an entrepreneur as it can be for an employee. Even though they work at different times, both groups end up having to sacrifice time for many things.

It's possible to have a lot more time for yourself by taking early retirement and having a solid plan in place to ensure your well-being in retirement. This is the time to accomplish all items on your bucketlist. It is fun because you can still do it while being active and young. Early retirement allows you to travel the world and enjoy your time, as well as enroll in the sport training you always wanted.

To avoid stress and anxiety that comes with these tasks, it is necessary to set up a financial arrangement that guarantees money flow. While it is important to have the time you desire to do these things, your freedom to do them will only be as good as the money you have.

4. You are likely to face more financial difficulties in the future that you have now

You can't predict the future without knowing the past. With the changing times, financial needs change. There is every chance that the future will bring more financial hardships than what we have now.

Your faith in the future you have now is sufficient to give you optimism about the bright financial future you expect. However, does that provide enough security to bank on? No. It's not. Because the future is unpredictable, there is no way to know for certain. Do not let the knowledge that the future is uncertain scare you. Instead, make sure you have a comprehensive plan for your retirement.

Early retirement is a great way to make sure you stick with your retirement plan. It also allows for you to have the time and understanding to regularly review the plan to ensure that it keeps up with current events. Uncertain times are part of life.

But they're just a way to get there. The best way to handle these uncertainties is to plan your retirement.

5. You Don't Have to Depend on Social Security and Pension

Retirees often rely only on the pension or social security they have in place. While there is an area for social security in retirement, it is not the best. These two are not enough to give you the retirement of dreams, especially if you have lots on your bucket-list.

It is possible to address this issue by focusing on other strategies, which can guarantee multiple streams. Your social security and pension funds can be used to supplement your income. It is assumed that if you retire early you are still vibrant in your thoughts and actions. Both can be used to transform your entire life.

To make the most from early retirement, you will need a plan. An adequate plan can provide a safety net that meets all your needs, until you are ready to leave this planet.

6. It allows you to find meaning and fulfillment

For many, working is just a way for them to get a living. Your passion might not match what you earn. Earning money doesn't guarantee that you will be fulfilled by it. By planning well and working hard, you can make a plan for early retirement so that you can continue building wealth while not being employed.

Saving time from not working and the money from your savings and investment can be used to follow a greater path that is beneficial for humanity. You are likely to find fulfillment knowing you make people smile and sleep well every night.

It seems that many people in this world are being challenged and disadvantaged. While the fortunate have the capacity to offer assistance and contribute their part to societal development, the rest of us seem to lack the time. When you retire properly and early, you will be able to join the ranks for outstanding people who leave work to engage in activities and movements which enhance society. You'll find fulfillment every minute you spend doing it.

7. You have all the time you need to be a part of and contribute to your family

Work can be very draining on your family. You may not have enough time or the right kind of work to spend time with your loved ones, depending on what you do. Many people have to relocate from their home city to continue their jobs. You may not have enough time to take a family vacation.

You can retire early and still be part of your family. You will be able to spend more time with your spouse, and you can go on many vacations together. You can be a part of your children's lives and actively participate in their raising. You can be there for them at work and school, providing all the support they require.

You don't have to make excuses for not attending family outings and meetings. You can embrace your loved ones and family more by retiring early. While work is wonderful and money is awesome, there's nothing better than the feeling of loving, being loved, or getting to spend time with your family whenever you wish.

8. With proper planning and early retirement, you don't have to rely on your family.

Many people retire and are left to rely on their families for their entire lives. This is due to two main factors: late retirement and poor planning for retirement. If you don't have a plan in place to support yourself in retirement, it is more likely that you will be dependent on your loved ones or family for survival. This can be avoided by taking early retirement. You have the mental and physical strength necessary to carry out the plan you have created to support yourself in retirement.

Proper planning and early retirement can make you a blessing to your family and friends, and not a burden. If you depend on your loved ones for survival, you are a burden. But, you can be a blessing if you support their dreams and aspirations with your finances and your thoughts, or both.

9. It allows you to focus on your health.

You have the opportunity to focus on your health and take early retirement. You might find work that is not good for you and your health. Your work schedule might make it difficult to take care of your health. You can relax and get the rest you need with early retirement. For regular checkups and health maintenance, you can continue to see your doctor.

You might find it difficult to exercise regularly due to your work schedule. This is a problem that can lead to poor health. You can change this when you retire.

As we have already said, early retirement is not without its difficulties. The bright side of early retirement is far more rewarding than its difficulties. There are some challenges associated with early retirement, such as insufficiency or the pain of doing something you love. It might be difficult to quit a job you love and feel fulfilled in if it is a challenging and hard job.

Regardless of how much you love your job you can't stay there forever. You will eventually have to retire. Your retirement will be interesting if you have the right plans in place. Your bucket list is already a detailed description of your goals and plans for the future. You don't have to wait any longer to begin planning to complete every item on your bucket list.

Financial independence is possible with early retirement. You need to know how to save money for retirement and how to invest to achieve financial independence. This guide will help you understand what early retirement means and how to prepare for it. It will also show you how you can build wealth that will supplement your pension and retirement benefits. Learn about common mistakes in retirement planning and how you can make the most out of your retirement.

Chapter 7: How To Retire Early

Traditional retirement planning is very similar to arly planning, with one exception: time. Early retirement planning allows you to reach your financial goals in a shorter time frame and your wealth will last longer once you retire. You have two phases: a short financial planning phase and a long post retirement spending period.

Most people can retire early. All you have to do is use the tools that you already have for financial success in an aggressive and strict manner. It may require a lot sacrifice on the part of most people. Everything must be done quickly, with little time.

Other aspects of retirement planning are also affected by a change in the traditional retirement age-frame. While all the traditional retirement planning processes still apply to early retirement planning there are certain aspects that have been magnified by the shorter time frame.

These are the essential steps you should take when planning for early retirement.

You can build assets faster

Conventional retirement planning relies on traditional financial strategies like passive investment and savings strategies. Also known as the slow, secure path to wealth, this is also called conventional retirement planning. While this is fine if you have a 40-year career and are looking to fund a 30-plus year retirement, early retirees tend to have shorter careers. This means they have less time to save and more money to spend when they retire.

Traditional financial concepts have a problem: passive investment portfolios are not as efficient for those who want to save money and retire early. Based on the analysis of data, long-term returns can vary from low to mid single digits net inflation. This is far below what is required to quickly grow wealth for early retirement. A diversified passive portfolio will typically have a 15-year period with negative real returns.

Let's be clear: if you want to save money and passively invest to reach early retirement at normal spending levels then think again. There wouldn't be enough time to grow the asset meaningfully. You can achieve this by incorporating non-conventional strategies into your plans. You must apply one or more of these principles:

Extreme Frugality is a rare type of saver who has low spending in comparison to their income. In order to retire within 7-10 years, people have been known as to save as much as 70% of their income. This is possible, but it can be very difficult to do.

Active Investing is an investment strategy that adds a skill element to the mix. This creates a higher return stream than passive investing. You can quickly increase compound returns with large investment returns.

Leverage: This refers to extending your resource base beyond what you can do. It gives you the chance to obtain more resources in a shorter time. This allows you to double your earnings in the same time.

This is not a popular path to early retirement. It requires investment skills and personal funds, which few people with regular jobs have. Real estate is a popular way to retire early because of its financial leverage, tax advantage and business leverage. It's also easy to learn. It is also easier to learn. Real estate often offers higher returns than passive investments.

These strategies are popular because they combine unusual value with skills and financial leverage to increase returns.

Leveraging other people's time by owning a company is another popular way to retire early. Businesses provide tax benefits and leverage that are not available to passive investors. You have the option to start your own business, or you can become the owner of a company through stock options and stock bonuses.

There are three main paths to wealth: real estate, business, and paper assets. Only two of these offer leverage (realty and business), which is sufficient for early retirement without extreme frugality. Traditional retirement planning uses paper assets, which is why it's slow.

Passive investment in paper assets is too slow if the goal is to create wealth that will allow for a secure and prosperous early retirement. This takes more time than a person who wants to retire early can afford. To reach financial independence faster, the best route to your goals is to use an active and leveraged asset collection strategy to get there sooner.

Plan for inflation

Inflation is similar to cancer. It reduces the purchasing power and value of early retirement savings. If you don't have the right plans, it can cause financial instability and a hidden tax on your wealth. This is especially important for early retirees, as it can take longer to cause damage if you retire early.

Inflation of just 4.5% will reduce your money's purchasing power by half every 16 years. To maintain your purchasing power, you will need to double your savings over the same time period. With an average inflation rate of 4.5%, a retired couple in their 40s could see their purchasing power fall by at least three times. An example: $100 worth of goods would cost $500 in 1960, but that's an annual compound inflation rate at 4.8%. This has completely destroyed 80% your purchasing power.

A retiree in 1960 would need to increase his retirement savings and portfolio five times to offset the inflation. This does not include the principal expenditure necessary to support living expenses and capital gains taxes. Inflation is a problem, not a solution.

It is misleading to say that nominal growth in assets is misleading. In the long-term, the only growth that matters is an increase in purchasing power. Passive returns from investing are often nothing more than inflation in asset prices. A retiree in their early years must be careful as inflation is essentially a tax on assets. The longer it takes, the greater the damage it can cause to your real wealth.

Fixed annuities and pensions which don't adjust for inflation are long-term disasters. Inflation effects must be offset by income sources and portfolios for early retirees. You can rent real estate, equities and fixed income sources that have cost-of-living adjustment provisions.

Spending issues

Conventional retirement planning calls for spending to decrease overtime as you get older. Because spending is directly linked to activity, which decreases over time due to declining energy and health, this is why conventional retirement planning requires that you reduce your overtime spending. This decrease in spending with age is helping to reduce inflation. Conventional retirees can enjoy a fairly balanced spending picture.

The opposite is true for early retirement. Early retirees' spending almost always rises and stays high due to their active lifestyle and good health. They cannot rely on lower spending to offset inflation as conventional retirees. To be financially safe, they must fit in one of these categories:

* You should not retire with more wealth than is necessary to maintain your current lifestyle.

* Retirees need to earn above-market returns in order to overcome inflation and other costs associated with retirement.

* Earned income can be used to support retirement income.

* Make lifestyle changes to lower expenses.

Many early retirees choose to join one of these four categories in order to make ends meets.

Be Self-Reliant

Conventional retirement has a three-legged stool that provides income. This includes pension, savings and social security. These are either reduced to one or two legs in early retirement. Because most early retirees can't qualify for Medicare and Social Security, Medicare is the missing leg. Eliminating government retirement programs places an additional burden on savings and income sources.

This means you need to plan for lower income at the start of your early retirement, before social security kicks in. You also need to plan for higher self-insurance costs until you are eligible for Medicare.

The time difference between conventional retirement and early retirement creates additional financial stress for early retirees, in terms of decreased retirement income and higher health insurance costs.

In order to retire early, you need to have a steady income without spending principal.

Planning for early retirement requires a steady source of income that you can count on. This is because a couple that retires in their 40s may have at least one spouse living to their 90s. It is basically a 50 year plan. Consider a 30-year traditional mortgage to understand the impact on spending principal. While the monthly payments for the first month contain very little principal, the payments for the second and subsequent years are almost entirely made up of principal.

The same applies to retirement living. While the first payments are very low in principal, the principal is used on the later payments. You don't know when your last payment will be until it's finished. This is the main problem. You don't know when your death date, so you have to assume that you will live to the fullest. An early retiree should not spend more than the principal until the end. By then it is too late.

This basically means that traditional retirement can only use a small amount of principal, while early retirement requires a stream of income that can grow over time to offset inflation. Although it's more difficult to implement, perpetual income planning is easier than traditional retirement planning. Planning for early retirement is not possible without using the different assumptions and estimates required by traditional planning.

It would be impossible to plan for an early retirement with conventional models, but it is possible with these simple rules.

* Create an investment portfolio that is sufficient to generate residual income above personal expenses. This applies only to residual income, not total return. Only income from assets can be spent, but assets cannot be destroyed. You can become infinitely rich if the cash flow from your portfolio exceeds what you spend on daily living expenses. Because you can't outlive your income, your life expectancy is irrelevant.

* Manage assets to ensure that their growth is greater than the inflation rate. This, in other words, takes care of the inflation problem. If assets such as property, dividend-paying stocks, or positive cash flow rental properties are where you get your cash, then they will grow along with inflation. You should ensure that your total return and income from assets exceeds the rate of inflation. This will negate the need to estimate future inflation.

* Make sure you have multiple sources of residual income that are not correlated. This requirement can be met by having

enough income-generating real estate and dividend-paying stock. You can add passive income from your business, royalty income and fixed annuity income to increase your pension income or social security income. It would be foolish to retire on only one source of income. Many airline workers were forced to retire on their pensions, which were destroyed by the bankruptcy of some airlines. They had no other options and either had to change their lifestyles or return to work.

* This rule is an insurance policy for the unexpected. If your passive income is less than your personal expenses, you should not take early retirement. This will ensure that you have money left over to invest. This insurance is an extra measure to protect against unexpected problems such as inflation and lost income. You can increase your recovery time from any circumstance by reinvesting excess revenue.

These simple rules, which do not require assumptions or calculations, make it easy to understand how early retirement perpetual finance works. These simple rules will ensure that you have financial security throughout retirement, no matter how old you are or when you retire.

What is the best way to get early retirement?

What happens to the 2000+ hours of work that you do each year once early retirement is over? An enjoyable early retirement involves more than just a life of leisure, such as playing golf or reading novels and watching daytime TV. The majority of people find that such lifestyles are not sustainable. The human brain is wired to be social, productive, and goal-seeking. Anyone who has the desire and drive to make his early retirement goals a success can easily give up on boredom by taking a full-time vacation.

It is a huge mistake to plan for early retirement without a good understanding of recreation, flexibility, freedom, or spending time with your family. You should feel excited about the possibility of a better and more fulfilling lifestyle if you decide to retire early. You should have a passion or an activity you enjoy. These interests should align with your core values and be something you are excited about. Financial advisors might consider starting a mentoring business to help them retire early. The knowledge and passion associated with finances will be a huge asset to him/her.

Some retirees combine part-time, volunteer, stint work and launching new businesses with the arts and other occupations to increase productivity and human connection in their daily lives. Some people spend more time at the gym to improve their health. Others use it to pursue their hobbies, such as flying or traveling.

You can combine them in any way that you like, as long as they make you happy. There is no right or wrong way to enjoy an early retirement filled with fulfillment. Everyone is unique and finds different things interesting. You just need a compelling reason to get up each morning that is more than your own self-absorption.

Retirement is not about full-time leisure, that's a myth. It is also a mistake to think that money should be the focus of retirement planning.

There are many benefits to early retirement, but there are also many issues. Particularly in the preparation phase. You have less time to prepare, and you will need more time after retirement. These issues can be addressed by following the steps. Each step can help you plan for early retirement and not be surprised by the harsh realities. You can achieve early retirement fulfillment if you follow the steps correctly.

Chapter 8: Financial Independence Is A Must Before You Retire

If you're already proficient in finances and are savvy with your transactions, you may be well on your way to financial independence. Financial freedom may seem impossible if you're struggling to get out of debt or just starting to learn the basics of managing your money.

There's no reason to be afraid. It's not necessary to be afraid.

Let's do an exercise. Get a notepad, an iPad or any other device that can be used to write. Good. Write down the top 20 things that will make you the most happy person on earth. These are the things that matter to you. These are the things you are passionate about. There are 20 things you can write about, so take your time and reflect on the most important aspects of your life. There is no pressure.

Are you done? Great.

Is there anything physical or tangible on your top 20 list, such as a designer shoe or mega-yacht? Is there something you cannot physically grasp but that still matters, such as time? More time. Do you feel irritated that you don't have enough time with your family and yourself?

You know deep down that these 20 things will make you happy when you retire. But what is stopping you?

You will be distracted by the hustle and grind of daily life. It is easy to get caught up in the grind of daily life. Before you know it, you will be surrounded by monotonous tasks like commuting, work, and just trying to survive. This will cause you to lose sight of what it means to live a happy, fulfilled life. It's okay. It's okay. Deepen your breath and declare that you will be financially independent before you retire.

This should be your daily mantra until you reach it. It is the key to happiness. All of life boils down to happiness and freedom. All you need to be conscious of is that your unconscious pursuit of happiness through all the troubles in life is the key to unlocking the door to happiness.

Both financial independence and happiness are good friends. Because you have the ability to access the former, it makes the journey to the latter much easier and more comprehensible. Financial independence will allow you to not only acquire the top 20 lists but also give you time for rest, family and, ultimately, yourself.

"But wait," you might be asking. "But wait, I understand. But what does it mean to be financially independent?"

The Fire Movement

The FIRE movement (Financial Independence, Retirement Early) is a lifestyle trend that began in 1992 after the publication of 'Your Money or Your Life'. The goal is to live a financially healthy life and save aggressively, with the ultimate goal of retiring in your 40s or 30s.

The basic idea behind it is to save a significant amount of your salary, approximately 50-70%, and then invest it in the hope that it will eventually reach a point where your earnings and expenses are comparable. You are considered FIREd when you have reached this point.

You have reached FIRE when you are able to make lifestyle choices that don't impact your financial responsibilities. You won't have to worry about working in undesirable jobs just because they pay more. FIRE will allow you to pursue your passions while also working part-time.

FIRE is for people who feel trapped, financially exhausted, or are constantly working and want to find an escape. Over time, the movement has been criticised for its inflexibility. Its basic steps will help you to reevaluate your financial decisions and make financial decisions that will improve your financial future.

FIRE advocates that you no longer need to work for extra money when you are retired.

Financial Independence

Financial independence, from the standpoint of someone who wants retirement, is the complete freedom that you have to quit the job you hate.

Let's say you quit your job and are now without a salary for a few weeks. You would probably be very well off. Most likely, you would be able survive on the savings money that you have. But what happens if your savings run out?

What would you do?

Would you like to return to your job?

Or would you take on another job doing the same 9-5 work that brought you to your knees and started you on your retirement journey?

NO!

No. This would be a defeat for your entire goal to reach your top-20 happiness-related goals.

Passive income is a powerful word that will allow you to say no.

You can live comfortably on passive income streams, and you can leave your savings account alone. This will make you financially independent. These goals will be possible to pursue with all your attention. Your life will be completely different and almost perfect.

Imagine it.

Imagine you were a happy person who enjoyed getting up every morning and that your energy was like four motivational speakers trying their best to lift the spirits of the crowd at a concert. Imagine you were able to pinpoint what makes you happy and that you worked hard every day towards that goal. Imagine that you were passionate about what you do, and that you could control every aspect of your day. Imagine that you didn't have to feel guilty about not being there for your children, your marriage, or your youth. Imagine financial security. You don't have to worry about paying the bills if you go out with your significant other. Imagine you could travel anywhere you wanted, whenever you wanted, with complete financial freedom. This is financial independence, my friend.

Financial independence is the first step to a life of unlimited freedom and early retirement. While the exact meaning of this term will vary depending on the individual, the essence is the freedom to choose.

You can do what you want with your time without having to worry about money or being tied to a job.

Financial independence can be achieved when you have enough passive income to cover all your monthly expenses. You don't need to worry about making money. This is critical to your early retirement.

A false sense of security in your job is Job security

This information is likely well-known to you, as you are reading this book. However, it is still worth noting. It doesn't really matter if your status is self-employed, owner of a business, or employee. The important thing to remember is that you are in the business of running it.

The customers they serve is what makes each one unique. If you are an employer, then your employer should be your primary customers. These people are the ones you give your time, skill, and services to. The other side is that if you are self-employed you will have many customers.

An entrepreneur will argue that having one employer is better than having several. Let's take this as an example. If your business is run entirely by you, then you will be able to find work. However, your customers would first have to 'fire' you before this would happen. The fate of an entrepreneur is not in the hands one single employer. This is the reason why it is crucial to be financially self-sufficient. There is no way for anyone with any skill, education or experience to guarantee job security, even for the most dedicated or skilled workers. The truth is that you as an employee are constantly auditioning for a job.

Escape the Rat Race Trap

We've already spoken about this in the previous chapter. The endless toiling, day-to-day work, and the unforgiving 9-5 grind. This is the 'Rat Race,' and it doesn't take me long to say how it can feel. This goes well beyond early retirement. The "Rat Race" is the evil and numbing passion killer that saps every desire for happiness and fills all available space for freedom. To be productive in all things and to achieve freedom in any endeavors that we choose, these are the goals which should not be sacrificed.

You can arrange work to suit you

Financial independence means you have more time and resources to pursue your passions, explore your hidden talents, and find ways to incorporate them into your work life. You will have all the resources and time necessary to make the most.

Even though financial independence may not be the only criteria for choosing the right type work, there might be a commonality. Research has shown millionaires tend to prefer work that is specific to their skill sets. This gives them an edge over the rest.

Your mental health will depend on the type of work that you do. While this can sometimes be overlooked, it will show up in your daily interactions.

4 Steps To Financial Independence

The First Step is to take control over your finances.

It is not difficult to get control of your money. Simply spend less than you make.

Although it can seem difficult to deal with the daily expense of living, it is important if your goal to financial independence is achieved. To begin, determine what your monthly expenses will be and then create a budget. The 50/30/20 approach to money allocation is a great option. It is essential that you know how to save substantial amounts of your income.

The second step in getting rid of excesses

We're halfway there now that you know what your monthly expenses are and how you allocate your money using 50/30/20.

It's time you get rid of all excesses from your budget. Financial independence can only be achieved if the money you spend isn't wasted. Although this may be difficult, it is important. Once you get rid of any excess spending, you'll be able to save more.

The third step is to increase and diversify your monthly income.

Once you have a healthy budget and are able to save money, it is time for you increase and diversify the income you earn.

Because you want to achieve financial independence before you retire, it is essential that you ask for a pay raise in any job you hold. Make sure you are prepared to speak with your boss. It is important to make sure that you get paid for what you ask. You also need to assess the current state of the company you work for. Make sure to let your boss know the things you want. Also, explain why you should be given a raise.

Additionally, if you have more time than you work, it is worth filling them with anything that will help your goal to financial independence. To achieve financial independence, you need to have multiple streams of income.

The fourth step is to activate your passive income

We've pushed it. You have no more time to make extra money. It is up to us to find a method to make more, without wasting any of the time we already have.

Passive income. This is the only and best way to earn more, without burning out. Making passive income is possible by investing the money you have been saving. If you make smart investments, you become an employer of the money. You don't even need to have a lot. No matter how negative you might be about the idea, the reality is that investing won't bring you more money. It is best to choose a low risk investment that will give you security and provide peace of head. When the time comes, play the long-game and you will see the results.

The Fifth Is To Take Action Now

It doesn't have be a drastic change in your daily life. You could work slowly and steadily to reach your overall goal. Important is that you do not wait. TIME is the first currency. Not money. Every second you spend deliberating on the subject is a wasted moment that could have helped you get started on your financial independence journey. It is tempting to set lofty goals. But, it will not get you there as fast. The best and most lasting results will come from small, steady improvements over time.

What does all this really mean?

It is possible to attain financial independence if you are persistent and willing to work hard. Some people attain it in their 20s while others reach it in their 30s. While some may be able to do so in their 20s, others might not before their retirement age. Many people who attain financial independence will work harder to earn more money. But the basic concept is simple: they won't ever have to worry anymore about money, their bills or what lifestyle they choose.

There are many methods to financial independence. Every method has its advantages and disadvantages. You decide the path to financial independence, and what techniques you use.

It is not a sprint. You must be steady and consider your happiness while you work toward your financial goals.

Chapter 9: Setting Your Financial Goals. Where, How, And Why?

You are on vacation and spot a charming residential building. What's next? You would like to recreate the design on the ground. It is not possible to have the desired house built on your land. The whole idea behind building the house of your dreams is lost!

Your financial goals after retiring are similar to that of the house. Uncertain of the reasons, how, or whereabouts of your financial goals can render them useless. The reverse is true. Robert Kiyosaki once remarked, "Financial Freedom is Freedom from Fear." A solid understanding of the intricacies surrounding setting financial objectives will lead to financial freedom. This chapter will break down each concept to help you understand the basics of setting financial goals.

Where do financial goals take root?

Financial goals represent one's financial buoyancy, which is quite fine. These goals are not etched in all areas. These areas offer fertile ground for financial objectives of any length. They can also be used as funding sources. If you want your financial goals to be successful, eliminate any distractions. You need to know where you can set your financial, and sustainable goals once you retire.

Set up an Emergency Fund

Retirement is like losing your job. An emergency plan that is set up during active work years will not make the situation worse. You don't usually have to withdraw your emergency funds before the deadline, but it can grow with longer time periods. The term "emergency", which means it can't be withdrawn for reasons other than sudden and accidental events, is strictly applied when disbursing this fund.

There are no excuses for not obtaining emergency funds.

Take a trip

The best health insurance

Long-term health care bills

Home and care maintenance

Giving assistance to adults and children.

How much cash to stash in an impromptu fund depends on how you live. These funds also exist in cash and bonds. The factors above indicate the amount of liquid you can use.

Multiplie income sources

Stakes

It does not mean that you are working on multiple ventures. You could be a shareholder in someone's business. If you find a successful business that you feel confident in and can win at, then buy shares. You will receive both interest and your investment, no matter how often it is. Everyone wins!

Part-time Jobs

A study showed that around 20% of retirees with an active career would be willing to accept part-time work. You could be part of this tiny group. This group allows you to work whenever and wherever it suits you. Pay attention to the benefits and good pay. You can also get health insurance and sick leave pay.

Social security benefits

A lot of retirees are attracted to these benefits. It is easier to appreciate this option if there are regular inputs over your agile years. As the benefits get more expensive, it is better to save them for the rainy times. Allow your social insurance benefits to continue growing once there are additional sources of income.

Pension funds

These are excellent investments that you should not overlook. You can make investments in pension funds as per your salary while you are in service. Pension money can be accessed via monthly or bulk payments when you reach retirement. Be aware of the high taxes on lump withdrawals when choosing your preferred method. Bulk money will allow you to pay immediate expenses while periodic payments may help your retirement budget. Pension funds, however, are great money storage.

Invest in Insurance Policies

An insurance policy - Yes, you should have one. Life insurance is what you want. This type is insurance will pay your insurer no money if you pass away. This is a great option for someone with dependents such as a spouse or children. The flexible policyholder insurance could cover payment for critical or terminal illnesses.

You can also purchase insurance policies that cover dental and medical care. It is common knowledge they can be purchased separately. This doesn't make dental coverage less important. Add it up.

Insurance can be purchased for travel by those who are passionate about adventure. This insurance will allow you to travel to new destinations. You also have the option of lifetime annuities or long-term health insurance.

Paying off your debt

You can stand out from the crowd of retirees who have accumulated debt. There are many kinds of debts. These include mortgages as well as credit and debit card obligations, borrowed money, and so much more.

Hypothecaries

Depending on your housing situation, the amount of mortgage money you owe could be significant. Because this is the beast that taunts most retirees, try to make your mortgage payment as soon as you can. To make your life easier, you can find a better and more affordable home.

Repayment of debt

It is crucial to refinance your debt in order to achieve your financial goals. Set up a repayment plan that is more manageable with your lender. So, your debts won't be burdensome and you can clear them at a comfortable pace. Refinancing terms that are longer and at reasonable interest rates will help you manage your debts well.

Card debts (credit/debit)

Card debts! A very real problem. It is almost an inexplicable urge to continue buying and buying until you realize the extent of your problems. Once you have taken a quick pause, you will see how much debt you have. This is a trap that must be avoided if one wants to maintain high financial standards. It's important to quickly get rid of your debts, and then make a vow to never fall for it again. For expert help, contact a reputable company to set up a credit counseling program. This program helps you to lower your credit card debt. You also get subsidy for interest and monthly charges. Overall, the consolidation program assists its participants in saving.

Lifestyle

Lavishness can be wasteful. This attitude should be abandoned when moving from regular monthly paychecks to payments. You should not spend your retirement money on unnecessary items and instead focus on what you need. Consider that takeouts from McDonald's are part your daily spending. Perhaps you would prefer to cook your own meals. This can help you save lots of cash. Additional aspects of one's lifestyle like fashion, entertainment, as well as housing must be considered. You eventually will find that you spend less and save lots of money.

You will be more inclined to explore all possible avenues to help you achieve your financial goals. It's time to start listing them. The goals will play a major role in any future endeavors. It is time to start writing. Next, you will learn how to set your financial goals.

How to set the right financial goals

These goals are more than just a list. They require thought as well as consciousness. In this instance, Shabby won't work. Each goal must be realized in a way that can be matched to the resources, actions, and conditions. Also, the act and repetition of creating a goal list will lead to every goal being achieved. We will now take a deep look into how to set financial goals.

List Your Goals By Preference and Importance

It is important that you have a scale of preferences when listing financial goals. Your priorities will dictate the order you want your goals to be placed. While long-term goals tend not to be prioritized over short-term ones, it is possible to make exceptions from time to time. However, no matter what kind of goal you have-- long term or short term, place them in order.

You can set your goals high

Financial statements are figures. Financial goals must be quantifiable. If you are aiming to accumulate at least $5,000 more life insurance each year, then you already have a minimum amount and an amount that you can work with. The amount you can put in a liter jug will be obvious.

Indicate your goals and set deadlines

It is not possible to be forever when financial goals are on the table. You should set a date and stop at which you can achieve your financial goals. Timing is not your friend. Don't delay achieving your goals. It is important to work hard and meet deadlines for goals. This will ensure that you are on track to achieve all your targets at the correct times. Constant reminders can be provided by sticking notes with dates, durations, and other useful reminders, such as on the fridge or on your desk.

Make a Budget

Yes, a spending plan can be set up to meet financial goals. A long-term goal can be, for example, feeding. When you have a predetermined budget, you have a guide and a warning. In addition to helping you maximize the allotted amount, the budget restricts you from spending more than is permitted. Refusing exercise of restraint could lead to other parts of your budget being affected, which can be very disastrous. It is impossible to avoid being disciplined--by using force.

Everyday, Work

You will find that your goals have deadlines that span months or even years. However, it is important to keep trying every day to make tangible progress. According to a popular saying, "Rome was not built within a day." Little drops of water create a powerful ocean. Your daily efforts continue to trickle towards your larger goal until it becomes a reality.

Keep an eye on how you perform

After you have put your goals into motion look at how well you are doing (your performances). Compare your plan to see if you are moving fast or slowly. The latter is not always good news. You should immediately note any loopholes which could lead to a slow journey to the final destination. If necessary, re-examine the entire plan and add additional initiatives. You must keep track of your goals as a way to accelerate their realization.

Make adjustments when necessary

Some cases are inevitable. This does not mean that you have to give up or abandon your goals. Unplanned events are possible and can lead to us spending more money than we had planned. It is worth the effort to add to your budget or cut back on spending where compromise is possible. These are necessary for unexpected situations.

Why should an impending retired person have financial goals

The narrative has changed. Previously, you were rewarded for your statutory workdays with immediate pay that helps to pay your bills. The curtain has been pulled back on a career, and you are ready to enter retirement. An excellent financial position is what every retiree wants. These are the top reasons to have financial goals after retirement.

They are a source of foresight

Setting financial goals is like planting the seeds for your future ventures. Some people might have one venture to finance in addition to building money. It could be a vacation. You won't feel overwhelmed if you have cash. You will always be able, no matter what the occasion, to have the cash you need to pay any expenses.

They Facilitate Focus

If a person is hungry, they don't have to think about eating. Food provides the basic need for hunger, and eating does not require any dangerous skill. The same holds true for you. Your worries can be significantly reduced when money is available. The next step is to learn how to make financial resources work for you to purchase other things. A retired banker may want to set up an accounting practice. He will need a place to live, to employ workers and to purchase the necessary materials to support daily transactions. He will need sufficient capital to get the necessities he needs without delay.

How to Save Money

You can use this information to help determine how much you need to save or invest. With your financial goals in mind, you can now ask yourself: "Can my debt balance in all forms assist me in achieving these goals?" It helps you avoid going on an unplanned adventure that ends up leaving you stranded. It won't make the experience go away in a hurry.

Financial goals require different strategies

Different strokes for different folks. Financial goals can be extremely different in their execution. To achieve your financial goals, there are different strategies that you can use depending on their extent. Some of these strategies include cutting back on expenses, investing, saving, and making sure you pay your insurance premiums.

Post-career Opportunities Assistance

No matter how unrelated or related to your career, starting your own business after retirement is a popular option. Others may venture into part time jobs. Your financial goals will influence your choice of work. Your choices in work will depend on how much money you can afford. If you have a goal that requires just enough money, a part time job is right for you.

Retirees with a sense fulfillment will be rewarded

Fulfillment, one of the greatest feelings you can experience in life, is one that I find most fulfilling. Ever seen a young person build a sandman by the beach, or create a snowman at Christmas. The bright red smile that he has on his face when he achieves his goal is a sign of immense joy. These are signs of fulfillment.

It will be easy to set goals and make it a priority to work towards them. To get sound sleep, start with the daily goals.

American bestselling author Dennis Waitley stated that it wasn't in the pursuit or happiness that we find fulfillment. He said, "It was in the happiness-of-pursuit."

This is the definition of fulfilment. Instead of trying to attain happiness, focus on reaching your goals. This will assure fulfillment.

However, financial goals can't be ignored. It is an integral part in a prospective retiree's life, particularly if he desires secure finances. Here are some of the options available for achieving your financial goals. There are many avenues available to help you get out of debt. These steps are essential for setting realistic goals. These goals should be set in order of importance, take into account the quality of measurement, have a budget assigned, receive indulgences, and be reviewed from time-to-time. These tips will ensure you have a fun and seamless experience. The long discussion on goal setting is over. People do not do things without purpose. Everyone who has financial goals should know why they're important. Financial independence and financial goals are crucial to financial independence in retirement.

Chapter 10: Everything You Need To Know About Saving For Retirement

After many years and excellent service, you might decide it is now that you are ready to retire. Your retirement years should be full of fun and joy. But, you must have enough money to back it up. If you do not have a lot of money, it is important to save for retirement.

It will be disappointing to learn that there will not be any income after so many years. People plan to travel, see the world, and have the opportunity to live the life they dreamed while in service. However, they cannot do this because they have not saved enough to retire. The negative consequences of not saving for retirement are often hard to overcome. Many retirees would not be able to find the job that gives them the life they desire after retiring. It is important to continue working if you plan on enjoying your retirement years.

These are just a few of the things that you would experience if you didn't save for retirement.

1. No "retirement."

You don't get to retire if your plans for retirement are not in place. Even if you worked for years, your savings plan was not in place to make sure you're able to retire comfortably. The company that you work for will not support you until you die. Now you're left with your achievements over the years. In the absence or a substantial retirement account, you work until you are dead.

2. Debt! Debt!! Debt!! !

It is possible to not save enough for retirement due to the way you live and the decisions you make while serving. If you live a life in which you have everything but no savings, you'll need to borrow money for specific bills and to meet your responsibilities. Without a retirement account, you will end up with more debts than you can pay off, which could lead you into a hole.

3. Loss in Shares and Properties

If you were able gather properties while getting paid salaries, it is a good idea. But without a retirement fund, your shares and properties could be lost. It is possible to lose the property that you used as collateral for loans. In some cases, you might opt to live a minimalist life due to lack funds for retirement. You might have to sell the apartment you live in and move into a smaller house.

4. Financial and emotional stress

As he accrues more debts, he also has to pay bills and fulfill responsibilities. If you do not have the financial resources required to meet all these obligations, you will become financially stressed as well as emotionally stressed. This could have a negative impact on your relationships with family and friends, as well as your financial health. If you do not have an exit strategy, you can cause stress in your family.

5. Loss Control of Your Future

When asked about their retirement goals, people often answer with "live life to the fullest", making their own decisions, traveling, and enjoying the freedom that comes with it. But, without a retirement account, you can lose all of these things and have no control over what happens in the future.

How to start saving money for retirement funds

We have already highlighted the risks of not having retirement savings and retirement funds. However, this section would focus on saving for retirement.

a. Start Early

To save for retirement, you don't need to wait until your retirement to start saving. It is better to begin saving sooner. If you have a job at the time, you can start saving as early as 25, or as soon as possible. The idea behind saving early is to be able to save or invest less money over time, and then make more profit. Young people have less responsibilities than older adults. So it's better to start saving early and invest while you're still young. Invest only in assets that are likely to produce earnings.

There will be some difficulties at the beginning. This is mainly true if it's your first time saving.

b. Start Small

It is a good idea to save little for retirement. This is because it takes discipline and consistency to save money. Smaller amounts are easier to manage. It is essential to make saving for retirement a continuous process. You can save small amounts every month to begin with, and you can increase your savings as time goes by. It's easy to get confused by the question, "How much should you save?" 15 percent of your income is a good start. This can be increased according to your convenience.

c. Choose an Brokerage Firm

While it is fine to manage your savings on your behalf, it is more beneficial to work with a brokerage to help you invest and trade securities. Large mutual fund and brokerage companies offer many account options. These accounts can be opened without a fee or with a large selection of investment options including ETFs and mutual funds. These brokerage houses also offer personal advisors to help you with investments.

You need to take time to research and consider all aspects of a brokerage before you make a decision. Changes in brokerage firms can have a negative impact on your savings. Therefore, it is important to take the time to consider all investment options and make informed decisions before making any decision. Don't pay too much attention to trading.

d. Be a Realist about Risk

An investment is one way of increasing retirement funds. Investments have risks. It's common knowledge that there are high and low risks. As such, it is crucial to think about how assets might affect your retirement funds and be realistic about what you can afford to lose. When you start saving money, you might not have a lot of money. You shouldn't deposit too much money into a savings account. The money will not pay you much in the near future. It is important to avoid investing in biotech or gold at the beginning stages of saving. ETFs/mutual funds are the best way to save money at the beginning stages.

Initial Investment

Knowing the best investment options when saving for retirement funds is crucial. ETFs as well as mutual funds might be an option for you if you are an early saver. ETFs as well as mutual funds have the advantage that you can invest any amount. Investors can take advantage of the active management provided by a fund manager to their mutual funds.

Additional tip for Mutual Funds: It is important to consider the performance of mutual fund investments. An ideal mutual funds would have a better overall performance and less lost money.

While most mutual funds will limit how much you can invest, ETFs should be purchased at the very beginning of your investment. Here are some examples:

* Invesco Dynamic Value Large Cap (PWV).
* SPDR Dow Jones Industrial Average - DIA
* SPDR S&P Dividend
* Invesco S&P 500 Pure Growth (RPG)
* SPDR S&P 500 (SPY)
* Vanguard Dividend appreciation (VIG).
* Vanguard Value (VTV).

* Vanguard Total Stock Market
* Vanguard, FTSE All World Ex-US (VEU),
You can choose to buy these ETFs at your convenience.

f. Know when to Accumulate Further

You will find it easier to save if it becomes a way of life. Once in a while, you'll be able increase the amount of money that you can save in a given month. You may be able, if your monthly earnings have increased or your investments are starting to grow more, to look into additional investment options.

You are more likely to make higher investments if you have more money to put into investments.

g. Get to Know Your Investment Options

Many retirement accounts can be used for retirement savings. For example, 403(b)'s, 457s, I.R.A.s, Roth I.R.A.s, 401(k)'s, Solo 401(k)'s, etc. Many people do not know the basics of how these accounts work. We will be addressing this problem now.

It would be better to understand that these accounts are affected by where and how you work.

1. If you work for profit-oriented organizations

An employer may offer a 401k as an account. This is how it works. You choose the plan by filling out a questionnaire that allows you to indicate the percentage of your income that you wish to save. Your employer then has the responsibility to deposit the money into a company. This is usually done automatically. You may also opt to increase your savings rates if necessary.

What you need to know regarding 401(k).

The best thing about the 401(k), is that it doesn't have to be taxed. This plan has tax advantages, meaning that savings contributions aren't subject to taxes until retirement.

Merit: The Merit plan is an automated one. Your contributions are accordingly scheduled. It is also tax-free. You can invest this money and not pay any tax on the profits. It also comes with employer bonus match money.

Demerit - There is a penalty for taking the money before retiring, unlike other plans that allow you access the money only for reasons you have deemed to be qualified.

2. If you work for a nonprofit organization

Employees of non-profit organisations usually have more account options. These accounts include: 403(b), 4057(b), plans, and401k.

What are the facts about 403 (b)?

The 403b plan is similar in concept to the 401k plan but it is not available to non profit organizations such as churches and charities.

Merits : The advantages of the 403b plan are very similar with those of the401(k).

Demerits

What is 457(b).

The 457b plan is identical to the 403b plan.

Merits: These are benefits that are similar to 403(b), 401(k), etc.

Demerits. The 457B plan does not offer the employer bonus match money. Withdrawing cash from this plan to pay for an emergency is much more complicated. It can also be associated with the other negatives of 401K.

If your self-employed or the organization you work for does not offer an insurance plan,

If your company does not offer retirement plans or you are selfemployed. These accounts are I.R.A. S.E.P., Solo401(k), Roth I.R.A. These accounts are available at large banks as well as brokerage firms.

What you need know about Traditional I.R.A

The traditional IRA plans are similar to the 401k. It is tax advantageous and income from the account is not taxable unless the account holder withdraws the funds after retirement.

Merits - The traditional I.R.A provides a wealth of tax benefits. You won't be required to pay any tax until you are retired. It is more flexible than the 401K, and allows for unlimited investments. You can purchase stocks, bonds or real estate.

Demerits. The traditional I.R.A can have some drawbacks. For example, there are penalties if you withdraw the money before retiring and that you must invest it yourself. An investment advisor is recommended for individuals with this plan before making any decisions about what investment to make.

Here are some facts about SEP I.R.A

The SEP I.R.A. as well as the traditional I.R.A. have similar functions. The major difference is that SEP I.R.A works for employees working at small businesses. This plan allows only the employer and employee to make the contributions. This plan is sometimes called a profit-sharing program.

Merits - This plan is an "everybody loses" scheme that benefits employees and self employed individuals, especially in cases where the contribution limits can be higher. You can also access money easily.

Demerits: Uncertainty about the amount of money that would be accumulated is a part of this plan. A penalty is usually applied to early retirement cases where the money is withheld. Additionally, it is possible to view the easy availability of the money as a problem.

What should you know about Roth I.R.A

Roth I.R.A. - This is a brand new form of I.R.A. It offers tax benefits and certain tax benefits. However, this plan allows for contributions that are made after tax has been taken. This means that income will be taxable but not taxed if it is taken out of the retirement fund.

Merits: Roth I.R.A. plans allow you to avoid tax after retirement. You can take your contributions from the Roth I.R.A plan without being penalized and it is flexible. The Roth I.R.A plan's flexibility makes it one the most desired retirement plans.

Demerits - These are cons that are similar to traditional I.R.A. You can also seek out advisors or invest yourself.

Solo 401K: What do you need to know?

This plan is meant for business owners, and their spouses.

Merits - The solo 401k is better for employers without employees as they can contribute more to it.

Demerits (or a demerit): It's more complicated and requires lots paper work. If you are planning to have employees, it is likely that you will need to alter your plan as the single 401(k plan would not work.

This chapter should have been able highlight everything you need know about saving for retirement. Not all savings plans are created equal. You may have to explore different options before you discover the best one. Enjoy years of enjoyment after retirement by making saving a habit.

Chapter 11: How To Invest For Retirement

It comes time for everyone to let go of their working gloves, no matter how hard you've worked the last few years.

As we all know, retirement is inevitable. So you should plan your life so you have something to fall back onto after your paycheck stops coming.

You may be retiring permanently or partially, but there's one thing certain about retiring: financial security is not the same as it was when you were 100% committed and dedicated to your job.

You can retire with financial security and the ability to still accomplish your goals.

The answer to your question about whether it's a bad idea to retire is "Yes". It's possible to retire in a bad manner!

Retirement comes with a lot. These people believe that retirement will reduce their expenses, and therefore make little to no effort in making themselves financially secure.

How do your Expenses Change or Increase when You Retire?

The mistaken belief among workers is that their costs will automatically fall when they retire.

This belief is based on the idea that when they retire, they'd spend less on travel to work and on clothes expenses.

This might be true to an extent, but it doesn't mean that there aren't other expenses associated with retirement. For example, shopping trips, car loans and home loans to cover taxes as well as children's education and upkeep.

These expenses are what will ensure that your expenses don't go down when you retire. However, they can rise, and if this happens, you could find yourself in a financial crisis.

Sustainability Plans for Retirement

Funds can be obtained through donations from loved ones, family members, and the state and occupational Pensions.

You can also make money by selling products and services to help you sustain your retirement income.

When you retire, there are many ways you can earn money.

Although these activities sound like fun and adventurous, there are downsides.

One disadvantage to these activities is that they can make you exert your energy, work you up, and make it harder to adapt to a new niche. This defeats the purposeful of retirement.

While you may think that these are all good options, it's important to recognize that they only have advantages if you choose to do them.

The second drawback of being an entrepreneur is when you stop working. If you go into any business "business" because you want to make a lot of money, then it's not right for you.

This is due to the fact that starting a business is not always as lucrative as it seems. If you want to retire, this will be difficult.

After you cancel your businesses, you only have one option for sustainable growth, which is INVESTMENT.

Why should retirement investing be considered?

You can reap many benefits from investing for retirement.

There are many reasons why you should invest in retirement. The first is to be financially secure when you retire.

Furthermore, saving and investing a portion of your income can help you reduce how much you spend. You will also be more honest with yourself if there are any unnecessary expenses that you have to pay.

This is why it's important to make a habit of saving some of your income. It will help you reduce unnecessary expenses.

The goal of saving a portion your income to invest in an investment account is to not only curb excess spending while you are still working, but to also make sure that you have something financially solid to depend on at retirement.

Also, you can earn more money by investing and saving for retirement via the Compound Inflation medium.

Compound Interest is a way to make sure your last years are as good as your King's. It allows you to save so much money and invest so much.

To top it all, you should also invest in retirement because your savings and investments will help reduce your tax liability.

Consider this: If you earn $50,000 a month, then your tax relief will have been taken. A percentage of your $50,000 savings will be used as retirement savings.

However, if you aren't on any retirement savings plans or investment plans, your tax relief won't be deducted. What will be left, which will naturally be a large amount, will be subjected a tax. This will reduce the net income (or your take home) by a significant portion.

You see, investments and retirement savings help ensure that you have a net income even after tax.

Take up a retirement savings plan or invest plan to get many perks.

What amount can I invest to my retirement account

This is a crucial question for many workers. Deducting a percentage from your income and placing it in a retirement plan account can be difficult and time-consuming.

You have more financial responsibilities than you can handle and less money to save. It's clear that you will need to invest a significant percentage of your income in retirement savings or investments.

It doesn't really matter how hard it is, it's something you should do in order to ensure your financial stability when you retire.

Recalling the question of how much your income should go to your retirement account, the short answer is that you can only let go as much as your budget allows.

It is your last chance to spend retirement like a mafia boss. This is why you should do everything possible to work towards it.

These four factors help you determine how much of your income to save for retirement.

Taken together, these are the factors that will make it clear that you must have as much retirement savings as possible to enjoy a financially stress free retirement.

This is the logical part. However, it's enough to save 15% on your income if your efforts are not significant.

Cnbc.com studies show that an employee with a gross income of $22,000 to $68,000 could invest 15% of this income into his retirement fund. This allows him to withdraw up to $1.3million to supplement his retirement income.

Please remember that your 15% contribution will not be the sole thing going into retirement. Your employer may also play a significant role in ensuring that this happens (if you are part of an employer-sponsored or defined-contribution plan like the 403b/401(k).

Employees can put a percentage of their income into a retirement plan, such as the one offered by the 401 (k) plan. This retirement account is set up by the employer.

The best thing about an employer-sponsored pension plan is the fact that, while the funds grow interest and accumulate interest until the employee reaches retirement age, they are not subject to tax.

This employer-sponsored plan for retirement is great because the employee doesn't have to pay the entire cost.

Employers are required to match the contribution of employees by contributing a portion.

Employers are required to match (or increase) the employee's contributions to their retirement plans through the Matching Contribution program.

Employers decide what percentage to add. This is up to them. While 50% of contributions are usually matched by employers, some employers can choose to match 100%.

Defined–Contribution plans and Defined–Benefit plans have a vast difference. While both plans are employer-sponsored, although the former is what I have just described, the latter, also known under the name of a pensions plan, allows employers to give employees this benefit based primarily on their income history, retirement age, and work experience. This type of benefit does not require the employee to make any contributions. This is the responsibility of the employer.

The above explains that you will need to invest and save a significant portion of your income to secure a match from your employers and eventually withdraw a "harvest".

What time is right to invest in retirement assets?

From the last subheading, you can depict that to achieve a comfortable and financially-sufficient retirement, you need to commence your retirement savings and investments as early as you can get on it.

The earlier you save for your retirement, the lower your percentage contribution. Also, your funds will grow faster, which in turn will result in higher retirement income.

If you wait until you're in your 40s or 50s before you fund your retirement account you may not get the financial security you need for retirement.

You need to begin saving and investing as soon as possible. This will allow you to have a long time to save as well as to grow your retirement funds.

In addition, you can enjoy compound interest on both your savings and investments by saving early. Start saving early to increase your interest rate and make more money. !

Do not forget to mention the fact that early investments allow you to recover any financial losses from your investments.

Start early and even if losses occur, you still have time to recover your finances and get on the right track with your investments.

Final word: Just like early birds get a worm, early savers have an advantage in making as much money for retirement savings than the late savers. !

Make wise decisions and begin saving right away! !

Chapter 12: Investment Channel

You've read many chapters on early retirement and investing. In this chapter, we'll be discussing different investment channels and help you choose wisely to save for retirement. There is no universal method for selecting the right investment channel. You need to be aware of three key points if investing is something you must do.

* Your investment must be capital that is maintained
* It should be liquid
* This is a good investment.

However, many investors have discovered that some investment channels which are profitable are entirely focused on digital currency investing. Although bitcoin was once a bad investment since it did not meet the three criteria, it is now a well-known investment channel.

There are investors who see the return as a quick and easy one, but don't think about the possibility of losing money. It is because most people search for profitable business investments which can double their investment quickly. In most cases this investment fails. The truth is that investing has both risks and rewards.

As you try to find the best investment channel, be sure to match your risk profile and that of the product. Some investments carry high risk and have very high returns. However, low-risk investments provide lower returns. It is vital to choose which investment is right for you. In this vein, we will present a list that includes some investment channels. But, before you start looking, remember that investment products are classified into two groups: financial assets, and non-financial.

Direct equity

There are many types and varieties of stock available. Picking the right stock may be challenging. Stock is also a volatile asset without guaranteed returns, which means that not everyone is interested. It is one thing that you decide to invest, but it is another to choose when to buy or when to exit. Although stock investing can seem like a tunnel opening, it is actually easier than you might think. Equity has higher returns than any other stock.

Because of the high risk involved in selling your stock, such as losing all of it or a significant portion, you may choose to use the stoploss method to help limit your loss. In order to use the stoploss method, you will need to place an order in advance to sell your stock at a particular price. In order to minimize the risk involved, you can diversify your portfolio and invest in different stocks and sectors. To invest in equity, you should open a Demat bank account. You can sell and buy your shares. Equity is a high risk investment channel with a higher return.

Banks

Fixed deposit banking is considered to be one of the best ways to invest. This is especially true for Indians. You will get interest on your fixed deposit money quite often if you put it there. For example, the Indian deposit insurance and credit guarantees corporation established a rule that each depositor was to be covered up to Rs 5 million. This started in February

2015 and covers both principal amount and interest. After the initial Rs 1 lakh insurance coverage, the Rs 5 limit was raised to Rs 5. You will have to choose your investment term in order to invest in a fixed-deposit. You can leave your capital there monthly or annually, or you could leave it there for half a calendar year or quarterly. You decide what works best for you. But, it's important to know that the longer your investment is in a fixed deposit the more interest you earn.

Although it is safest to invest in a bank, it is nice to still invest half of your savings there.

Digital currency

Another great investment channel is digital currency. This has been a huge success in the past few decades. There was a time when bitcoin investing was bad because it offered little or no return. And then, in the last few decades, it was completely unsuccessful. Recent years have seen bitcoin grow in popularity. This makes it a great option for investors. It's just like the stock exchange, which can fluctuate, so the bitcoin investment channel too. Because the currency doesn't have any value, it's not stable and very risky. You shouldn't be discouraged though, as the world is growing rapidly and everything has gone online. That means that even the cryptocurrency will become very valuable and you can make high profit from it.

Also, you will need to learn how to manage the business. This is because even though the interest rates are attractive and tempting, it could be difficult to recover.

Savings plan for senior citizens

Many retirees look for an investment channel. One option is to invest in a senior citizens saving scheme. This savings scheme is available for seniors as well as early retirees. You can access this saving scheme from any bank or postal office. However, it is only for those who are over 60. The senior citizen savings plan has a five year tenure. You can extend your term by adding another three years, but this can only be done once your scheme is fully matured. The investment limit may not be suitable for you but you can get more than one account. The interest earned on your savings plan can be paid quarterly. It is fully subject to taxes. Once you have made your investment, your interest rates remain the same up until your scheme matures. But, then, the interest rate is subjected quarterly review.

Real estate

Investment in real estate is a popular channel for investing. More people are choosing to invest. A lot of people mistakenly think that the house they own is an investment. It is not. The house they bought is their home. But you could make another investment if the property is acquired. You can make a profit by buying a property that is in a desirable location. If you decide to invest in real property, you can be sure of two incredible returns. The first is the appreciation in your property and second, the increase in your rent.

It is not without risk. One risk is getting permission from government to put up your property as a rental. This can cause real estate to appreciate very fast. However, eventually your property's value may drop below what you paid when you bought it. Real estate can be very exciting. Unfortunately, nobody ever really notices when trouble hits paradise. It's very difficult to bring up your property's original value if it falls.

Gold

The investment in gold is a wonderful investment channel. It is highly valued and provides high investment returns. But, buying gold is something to be cautious about, especially if you are purchasing it in the form of jewellery. It is different to buy gold than to make it. This can also be nearly as costly as the purchasing power, especially if you have an exclusive design in mind. You have two options. One, you can invest in gold coins that you get from the bank and another is to own paper gold. The latter is less expensive. Paper gold investment can be made in a stock trading market with gold as the asset. A sovereign gold bond or mutual fund is another option for investing in gold.

However, investing in gold is not without risk. The Federal Reserve may raise interest rates, or a conflict could cause gold to lose its value.

Pension system

A pension can be described as a long-term investment plan. It is an investment that you start to make while you're working. The national retirement development program is a mix equity, fixed-deposits, government funds, etc. You have options when it comes to investing in the retirement system. These choices are also dependent on your willingness to take on risk.

Securities

The stock market is a good investment option that is very profitable. While the stock market has its moments of decline, it is still a highly lucrative investment. The stock market has been growing steadily over the years. However, it is not stable and is subject to market forces. Security investment is a wise choice as it meets all the requirements of a good investor, including liquidity and profit. The stock market is large and offers investors plenty of opportunities. Market is very attractive because there are many companies that sell shares. It is as exciting as the stock exchange might seem. However, the market has a high level of risk. When shares fall, the value of your shares could be lower than what was purchased. This could result in a loss. But, if shares are priced high, you make huge returns on your investment. Investing is a great way to make an investment, but you have to see the good side.

Find a competent stockbroker to help with managing your shares. He will advise you on the best times to buy and sell shares in order to make a large profit. Your stockbrokers will always be able to read financial reports about the stock market. They will also understand how the business is being managed. Companies work very hard to raise the price of shares so that they can earn enough from them.

Equity mutual fund

Equity mutual funds look more like investing with equity stocks. To invest in equity mutual funds, you must have 65% equity and equity-related assets. If you want to invest in this channel you will need a fund manger who can help with trading your funds in a manner that generates many returns. Your equity plan can be classified based on the industry in which the investment was made and market capitalization. You can also choose to categorize it according to whether they are domestic or international stocks. Your manager will help you decide which one is best for you.

Debt mutual fund

If you are an investor who needs steady returns, then debt mutual funds is the right channel for you. It is less volatile than other investment options and can be considered safe. The investment of fixed interest in debt mutual funds is a form of fixed-interest investing that produces securities such as corporate bonds, treasury bills, and commercial paper. Before you make any investment in the debt mutual funds channel, it is important to understand that there are still risks. If you don't know much about the money market, you can find a manager who knows the stock market and can assist you with your investments.

Public Provident Fund

It is the preferred investment channel because of its longevity. You can invest for as many as 15 years. The compounding interest that you earn becomes tax-free each year. Because it has a sovereign guarantee backing system, public provident is a very safe investment. The best part about this investment channel is that the government regularly reviews the interest rate, making it more interesting.

Once you have selected the channel you want, it is essential that you fully understand its value and whether it is legit. Being an investor means that you need to understand that investing in stocks and choosing top-rated companies that offer a high price is risky. When the price falls, it can cause a drop in value. You need to be familiar with the market and avoid investing if your background is not in finance. If you do decide to enter the real-estate sector, you need to ensure that everything is legal and that it conforms to the local rules.

However, some of the above investment channels can be tied to fixed income as well as the financial marketplace. It does not matter which investment channel it is, but it is designed for wealth creation. They have the potential to offer high returns and high risk.

Any investor should not shun a promising investment channel out of fear. Instead, examine the process and evaluate whether the risk is manageable. Every venture into a business comes with its own risk. Multiple investments are important so that you can enjoy your retirement. However keep in mind the risks, tax, and time frames.

Chapter 13: Quit Your Job To Retire Young

It can be difficult to leave your job early in retirement. There are many things you should consider about how you live, what you will spend on your daily living expenses, and how much you can save for the future. You don't have the luxury of ignoring these things, but it is better to plan for them than to forget. It is better for you to retire early and face all the consequences. While early retirement comes with some challenges, it's better than late retirement if all of the major factors are accounted for.

Your decision is clear if you have considered it carefully and made the right decision to leave your job and retire early. Before you can quit your job early to make it a retirement decision, there are some things you should do. If you fail to take these things into consideration and address them before making the decision to quit your job, it could be difficult. You should consider many of these factors, but we will be focusing on the most important. What to do before you retire early?

* Have a Comprehensive Pension Plan

The quality of your pension depends on how comprehensive and complete your retirement plan. It is wrong to start thinking about a retirement strategy after you have left the job. A plan can be best drafted while you are still employed. You can complete your retirement by taking several steps.

This plan should detail the type and amount of activities that you want, as well as the places you would like visit. It should also contain how you intend on achieving each item in the plan. This is not an easy task. For some, it may take several weeks and others months. While you're still working, it might be necessary to regularly review your plan to make sure that it accurately reflects changes in your personal and professional lives. A comprehensive retirement planning is the first step to a successful retirement. It must be in place before you leave your job.

* Stop working and start saving money

If you already have a comprehensive plan for retirement, you will be able to see how your retirement will look. Although this picture isn't perfect because no one knows tomorrow, it does give you an idea of how your retirement will look. Every place and every activity you include in your retirement plans has a financial implication. It is also important to consider the cost of the plan before you start drafting it. Start saving while you're still working. You should create a savings program that will allow you to save a lot of money in order to be able to quit your job and get out of debt early.

There's a low chance you will be able to earn the same after quitting your job. The loss of income will have a negative impact on your savings, and you may not be able as to save as much. Savings can be difficult when you also have to meet the needs of extended families. As frustrating as it can seem, it's one of many costs that you have to face in order to make your early retirement comfortable and enjoyable.

* Live carefully and affordably

If you want to save a lot of money while still working, you need to live sparingly and be careful. Living frugally means you can cut down on the luxury lifestyle to help you reach your retirement goals. There are many types of stuff that you think you need right now, but actually you don't need. If you are serious about retiring early, you need to recognize and stop buying these things. Do not spend more while still working and your income is increasing. Instead, you should learn how to live a moderately comfortable life that suits your goals.

This does not mean your family must live in pain because you plan for the future. Living frugally simply means to enjoy the present while taking care of the basics, and ignoring the rest. If you do this, you will be able to save half or more of your salary.

* Plan for Future Expenses

Yes, you can set your early retirement age at 40, 45, and even 50, depending on your plans. You must plan your finances before you quit your job and retire early. At your current age, and likely when your job is done, you'll still be young, energetic, and healthy. This is not likely to be true until you retire. You will have to pay more for your kids' educations.

What happens if you become seriously ill and need a lot of money to pay for it? If you're looking for work after you retire, this is something you need to consider.

How do I plan for my future expenses? Doing something you enjoy is the best way to ensure financial security. This could be handwork and/or building on your existing skills or finding ways you can monetize hobbies. The future position of your family members, particularly children, is another consideration before you quit your job. If your children have not yet started college, it is important to plan for their tuition costs and other expenses.

* Pay attention to your investments

A common mistake early retirees make as they age is not being aware of the difference between savings, investments, and working while they do so. It's okay to save large amounts of your wages while still working. But investing is more beneficial.

Savings help keep your money constant in value, so long as you're not spending it. You may be eligible for a percentage boost from certain financial institutions. However, this is rarely a substantial amount.

Investments, on other hand, will help you increase the wealth of your savings. There are many investment strategies that you can use while working. This allows you to invest more than you would have if your only goal was to save.

The Myths About Quitting Your Job Early and Retiring early That You Should Avoid

There have been many myths that have been propagated over the years, including those about quitting your job to go into early retirement. Avoid falling for any one of these myths. You might find yourself in a difficult position. It is important that you identify these myths to help you avoid them.

1. Your Money is at Risk

One of the biggest myths surrounding early retirement and quitting a job is that money runs out. This is false. How much you have, or how much you will have in the future is not dependent on how many hours you work. It's possible for you to keep working and still run out. If you don't know the best ways to manage your money, you could end up running out of cash.

Good savings and investing are two great ways to ensure that you have enough money to get you through the transition to early retirement. It is possible to leave your job full-time and pursue other interests that you love, which will allow you to have money in retirement.

2. Your spending habits will change

To be able to quit your job and enter early retirement, it is necessary to cut back on spending. As we said, you must give up on luxurious living and focus your efforts on the basics. Many people feel this is a difficult area to be in and have created myths to make anyone who plans to retire early feel bad.

Living comfortably is not just about a good retirement. It is a fundamental requirement for anyone who has worked hard to earn their money. Not only is it something you should think about before quitting your job, but it can also be a habit to cultivate that can help meet financial goals or perform a task that you have assigned.

Numerous unforeseen situations can occur in retirement. How can you handle these situations if your savings plan does not allow you to cut down on your spending?

3. It Guarantees Permanent Happiness

Although this sounds positive, it does not change the fact of the truth that it is still a myth. If you believe that it guarantees happiness forever, and you plan to leave your job early, then you are wrong. Yes, you will feel a significant weight lifting off your shoulders.

It's not necessary to have a regular sleeping pattern that forces you to get up early in the morning to complete work. There wouldn't be any meetings or deadlines, so you'd have lots of time for yourself. But, these are not the only things that can guarantee happiness.

The first few months after quitting your job will be challenging. It will be difficult to give up the comfortable working life that you have lived for so many years and move on to a new lifestyle. It may mean you move away from your workplace and the co-workers you know. This can make it difficult for you. It's important to realize that although quitting your job in order to retire early is beautiful and a wise decision, it doesn't guarantee you happiness forever.

4. Boring, Early Retirement

Even though early retirement doesn't guarantee happiness forever, it isn't boring. Early retirement can be very interesting as it allows you to do all you want, and you have the freedom to accomplish everything you set out. You're still young and have lots of energy so you can dedicate all of your time to doing what you love.

The initial period after quitting your job can be dull because you are still trying out new things. You will eventually become comfortable with your new reality.

5. There's a chance that you could lose your identity, and even fall into depression

Many people have been taught that their identity is tied to the profession they work in. Because we work so hard, it is difficult to see beyond the work we do.

When you make the decision to leave your job in order to retire early, there is a myth that you might feel you have lost your identity. That is not true. You are making the decision to quit your job and to retire early because you love what you do. The best way to retire early is with a plan.

It is important to include fun things on your bucket lists. These are things that allow you to have fun and spend quality time with people you care about doing things you love. If that is the case, there are no excuses for falling into depression.

How to quit your job early and retire earlier

There are two things that can make it easier to leave your job and retire early: quitting because you don't find the work environment supportive or finding a job elsewhere. These tips will help you make it as friendlier as possible.

* Talk to Your Boss About It

You must talk to your boss before you plan to leave your job or retire early. Let your boss know you are closing the chapter on your life and opening a new chapter. Most importantly, let them know you took the time to think it through and that you believe it was the right thing to do. Recommendations: Thank them for taking the time to read this and let them also know that you are available in an informal capacity to help if needed.

* Make Sure Someone Is Groomed To Take Your Place

You should not just leave your job to take your retirement. Make sure you have someone to replace it. Make sure to inform management of your intention so they can put together a staff to take over when you're gone. It is important to make sure that you have the right person for the job so that you can replace them.

* Let co-workers know you will be leaving, and why

You want to be able to quit your job and end your career on a friendly note, both with your managers and your coworkers. Tell them you're leaving, and that it is not because of your job conditions. Let them know that you loved working with and learned so much from them. This will help to maintain a good working relationship with them when you retire.

Knowing what to do and what not to do is key to quitting your job so you can retire. Early retirement is beneficial in many ways. To start, you need to create a retirement plan, quit your job, as well as meet the requirements. Keep good relations with everyone at work when you leave. You might not need the job again but you may need them one day.

Conclusion

After looking through the entire guide, you'll be able to see that retirement planning is much more than just saving money to pay for your retirement. You should still have years to prepare for your retirement. You can make your transition to retirement smoother and more successful by using this time wisely. It's a good thing that you've already read this guide and thought about these pre-planning questions. This will allow you to stay ahead of many others soon-to become retirees. Never underestimate the importance a well-thought out retirement plan.

Follow the planning advice contained in this book. Continue to identify other areas of your life which may require attention before you retire. Your retirement plan will prepare your mind and ensure you don't forget any vital aspects. Your investments should be protected, and you must also take care of your health. To fully enjoy your retirement, you will need to have a strong financial plan as well as a strong body.

www.ingramcontent.com/pod-product-compliance
Lightning Source LLC
Chambersburg PA
CBHW061602220326
41597CB00053B/2072